BMX!
Bicycle Motocross
for Beginners

Other books by I. G. Edmonds:

Motorcycle Racing for Beginners
The Girls Who Talked to Ghosts

BMX!
Bicycle Motocross for Beginners

by I. G. Edmonds

ILLUSTRATED WITH PHOTOGRAPHS
BY THE AUTHOR

Holt, Rinehart and Winston / NEW YORK

Library of Congress Cataloging in Publication Data

Edmonds, I. G.   BMX! Bicycle motocross for beginners.

Includes index.
Summary: Discusses the competitive sport of BMX,
bicycle motocross, the newest thing in bicycle racing.
1. Bicycle motocross—Juvenile literature.
(1. Bicycle motocross. 2. Bicycle racing) I. Title.
GV1049.3.E35   796.6   79-4311   ISBN 0-03-044321-0

Contents

BMX!
Bicycle Motocross
for Beginners

1. Pedal Power!

Six hundred bicycles straddled by eager riders are crowded into the staging area. They are eagerly waiting for the start of a Grand National BMX—Bicycle Motocross—race.

BMX, run on bicycles, is the newest thing in two-wheel sports. It is a spinoff from motorcycle motocross, the most popular form of motorcycle racing in the United States today.

Bicycle motocross is a competitive sport that is strictly for young people. The rules are that it is open only to riders between the ages of five and nineteen. After that, the gate is barred and riders must graduate to other two-wheel sports.

At the nationals race we will follow, the youngest riders are six years old. Seven participants in the race are girls, riding in their own division. The rest of the riders are divided into age groups, ranging up through the sixteen-and-over class.

Motorcycle Motocross
Motorcycle motocross began in Europe when someone had the idea of shrinking a cross-country course and fitting it into a track. In cross-country racing, riders

plow through dirt, mud, and rocky ground, go through streams and up hills, and tackle just about any kind of land a motorcycle can get over.

Designers of the first motocross tracks kept this general idea. They laid out a looping course with both right and left turns. Then they put in jumps, water hazards, mud, sand, and other obstacles to match those that nature provides in cross-country racing.

Most races are run in laps. A lap is one time around a closed course. Motocross is different. It is run in *motos* instead of laps. A moto is a length of time. This may vary from fifteen to thirty minutes, depending upon the promoter who runs the race. The winner of a moto is the rider who gets around the track the most number of times in a moto.

The winner of a moto is not necessarily the winner of the race. There will probably be three motos to the race. Riders earn points in each moto. After all the motos, the rider with the most points is the race winner. It is possible to lose one moto and still win the race if you can come in first on the other two.

Motocross quickly became the most popular type of motorcycle racing in the United States. This is partly due to the variety in its tracks. As one enthusiast put it, "You don't just run around in a circle. You have to get in there and work to win." The same excitement and difficulty are part of bicycle motocross.

The Beginning of Bicycle Motocross

Sometime around 1972, boys with bicycles began imitating the faster ones on their motocross motorcycles.

This play led directly to bicycle motocross—or BMX, as it is called by the pedal pushers who have made it into a new sport.

Once eager kids started fooling around with BMX, it did not take long for the sport to get organized. By 1973, clubs and the first association were already underway, and girls began to join in the fun.

Today there are at least two BMX newspapers and a magazine devoted to the sport. The sports editor of the Los Angeles *Examiner* estimated that nationally at least 75,000 boys and girls are now participating in BMX. BMX club officials call this estimate low. They say the number is closer to 80,000, and that the total will top 100,000 within a year.

Regardless of who is right, there is no denying that BMX has caught the fancy of sports-loving young America.

At present there are an estimated 350 BMX tracks scattered across the country. New ones are being reported every month. And the way manufacturers are fielding their own BMX teams and building special BMX equipment shows that the people with the money are convinced that the bicycle sport is here to stay.

Differences Between BMX and Motocross

Although BMX began as an imitation of motorcycle motocross, BMX fans deny that their new sport is motocross's "little brother." They claim that their sport is tougher than motocross. "After all," they say, "those dudes have *horsepower* to move them along. All we have is *boypower*. That makes it tougher."

While BMX clubs claim to make their races as nearly like motocross as possible, a bicycle is not a motorcycle. This forces many changes in rules and procedures.

For one thing, the track is shorter. It may be as short as one-eighth of a mile, and is never over a quarter of a mile. Instead of the timed moto, BMX riders run one lap around the course. They still call it a moto instead of a lap, however.

In motocross, the motorcycles are classed according to the displacement of the cylinders (which is the volume of the cylinder in cubic inches when the piston is at bottom dead center). This ensures that riders compete only against machines of similar power.

But in BMX competitions *at this time* all riders must use bicycles with 20-inch wheels. This gives everyone an equal chance as far as equipment goes. Since power is provided by the legs of the riders, classes are divided according to age groups. This does not always make things even, however. Size and strength are not always as important as skill and the determination to win.

Age Classes

Some clubs have a different class for each year of age— one class for seven-year-olds, one for eight-year-olds, and so on. Others may group two age levels into one class. If there are not enough entrants in one age class they may let a younger rider run with an older group.

This happened at a California track recently. An eight-year-old girl had no one to race against. So they let her join the nine-year-old boys' class. They did this just to be nice (or maybe they did not want to refund her two-dollar entrance fee). Anyway, she ran—and came in second, beating out five boys older than her.

Not nearly as many girls enter BMX races as boys, but those who do race are tough competitors.

Tracks that classify riders by age insist on a winner showing a birth certificate before receiving a trophy. This is to assure that an older, stronger but small-size rider is not trying to pick up an easy trophy by running under class. Such a tactic is called *cherry picking*.

Basic BMX Rules

Some rules are standard at all tracks. This is to insure that this is a motocross race and not something else. However, unless a club belongs to an association that enforces standard rules for all its members, each racing club makes most of its own rules. These cover safety, eligibility, classes, and entrance fees.

Even in sanctioned races put on by associations local conditions may sometimes require rule changes. If these are necessary, the rule changes are explained at riders' meetings before a race.

This Is BMX Racing

Here is what you might see at a typical BMX race staged under sanctioning association rules:

Each rider pays an entrance fee, ranging from one to four dollars. This fee must be accompanied by an entrance form that has been signed by a parent. Participants must be between five and twenty years old.

A riders' meeting is held before the races to explain the rules.

These forms are sorted into classes. Lists are posted to let each rider know the class and moto he or she will run in. Boys and girls may run in the same races or there may be separate races for each.

Then a riders' meeting is called. Race officials are generally men. Women—usually mothers of riders—act as judges and scorers. The officials are fine gentlemen, but they are not always polite. Sometimes they are downright mean.

Here are the exact words recorded at one such meeting: "I want to say for the benefit of some of you jokers that we have these rules to give everybody a fair break. And to see that about half of you don't break your necks. Anyone who thinks he can get away with thumbing his nose at the rules is going to be booted right off the track. If this happens, don't come asking for your entrance fee back. You won't get it! And let me tell you this. . . !"

Race officials often act and sound like football coaches with rookie squads. Nobody seems to mind, for everyone knows that ninety-nine times out of a hundred the officials have good reason for being angry.

After the riders' meeting, those in the first motos roll their bikes to the staging area. This is where they wait for their call to the starting line. The starting line is usually built on a mound five feet or more above the

In the staging area young hopefuls wait for their turn at the starting line.

Riders line up behind a metal gate for the start. The downhill start makes for a fast race.

level of the track. This puts the riders up where the judges can watch the action better. It also gives the riders a sharp downgrade for a faster start.

Now let's go to the nationals race we will be following.

They're Off!

There are several methods of starting a race. Our race used a mechanical gate which was dropped by the starter to begin the race.

Riders in the first moto lined up behind the gate. The gate dropped and eager legs pumped hard on pedals. Bikes and riders shot down the ramp, cheered on by the spectators.

One rider tried too hard. He hoped for a fast start to

put him out in front. Instead, his front wheel came up in a *wheelie*. This slowed him down until he could get his wheel back on the ground. The others sped on past, leaving him in the rear.

The number-three rider did not have his wheel lined up straight for the start. This was because he was paying more attention to the other riders than to his own bike. He got off to a fast start, but came down the ramp crooked.

Realizing his mistake, he tried to straighten up, but did not see the rider coming up on his left side. The two cycles bumped. The other cycle wobbled, but kept on going. Our man almost spilled, but he got one foot down fast enough to keep his balance. By the time he got lined up again, the rest had passed him. He had

The gate drops and riders hit their pedals for a fast start.

been third a second after the gate dropped. Now he was Tail-End Charlie because of one mistake.

He set out in a mad dash to catch up, pedaling fast down the short straightaway between the starting mound and the first turn.

The corner is sharp and unbanked. All riders hit their brakes to slow down enough to avoid spills. Inexperienced riders brake too soon. Overconfident ones brake too late. Veterans know exactly how far they can go into the turn before they have to brake to keep upright. This lets them make the turn with less loss of speed. This is where experience begins to tell. They pull ahead of the more cautious.

Smart riders extend the inside foot on these turns, skimming—*hot shoeing*—the ground to help keep the bike from sliding out of control.

Spills and Thrills

One rider went into the corner too fast. He flopped, rolled over, and came up unhurt, but two riders coming in fast behind him did not have time to swerve. They plowed into his overturned cycle. Thus three riders were scratched from the race. Worse yet, the first rider's front wheel was bent so badly that it would have to be replaced before he could ride again.

This helped Tail-End Charlie. The pileup permitted him to regain some of his lost ground. He was beginning to run a pretty good race after his initial trouble.

The riders took another short straightaway, and then went into a left turn. This turn was banked. Such corners—aided by some hot shoeing—can be taken faster

Putting your foot out on sharp turns is called hot shoeing. It helps to keep your bike from falling. Note the bales of hay marking the course. They make soft bumpers if anyone runs off of the track. These racers are in the seven-year-old class at an NBA Nationals meet.

than flat corners. But too many tried for the inside—for they all knew that the inside of a curve is the shortest distance around a turn. However, if too many riders try for the inside, it can cause a traffic jam and hold up those in the back.

Using the Berm

Old Charlie was back far enough to see the leaders bunching up on the turn. He played it smart. He swung to the outside. Sometimes the longest way around is the shortest distance after all. Using the berm—the ridge of dirt thrown up by the wheels of earlier racers—Charlie hot shoed his way around the outside of the loop. This let him get ahead of several riders who had been cut off by the jam on the turn.

On BMX tracks, riders do not have much time to get used to anything, or even to take second breaths. This sport moves fast. After the turn there is a short straight to let everyone get strung out again. Then they all head into the first of a series of jumps.

Many novice riders get nervous when their bikes start flying. Not Charlie. He loves the feel of both his wheels leaving the ground. One rider, more cautious, slowed and just rolled over the jump mound. Confident Charlie charged up the incline as fast as his pumping legs could carry him. He intended to give the others a southern view of a northbound Charlie.

Flying Bikes

Charlie charged up the mound. At the summit he slipped back on the seat to put his weight on the back wheel. This brought his front wheel up as his back wheel sailed off into space. Old Charlie was making like a bird.

He pulled up his front wheel, to make sure he would land on his back wheel first. This helps absorb some of the shock of landing. Also, landing on a front wheel can bend a fork, bang up a wheel, or even throw a rider right over his handlebars.

When the back wheel of the cycle settled back to earth after its short flight, Old Charlie shifted his weight forward and pressed down on his handlebars to get the front wheel on the ground again.

Charlie's face was streaked with sweat and dirt now. His lungs were panting for air. His tired legs felt like they had been pumping for hours. Old Charlie was wishing now that he had taken a few more deep knee bends during his morning conditioning exercises.

Whoop-de-dos!

Things were looking good for Charlie. He was pushing the front runners now and had a fair chance of winning. There were only one straight, a jump, and a stretch of whoop-de-dos between him and the finish line.

Charlie had fought himself back to third place again. This was good, considering his bad fumble at the beginning. He felt that his good jumping technique would put him in front at the next mound.

Sad to relate, races are run on the track and not in a rider's imagination. Charlie got boxed in on the jump. He could not get around the other riders. There just was no hole to charge through.

Then on the straight there was a mud hole, but since they all had trouble with it, Charlie came out of the soup still in third place. Then he moved up to second on the final banked turn by taking the corner too fast. Good luck—instead of good sense—brought him through.

He was in the final stretch now. He could see the flagman waiting to wave the checkered flag for the winner. It would be himself, he was sure, for he had only two problems left to overcome. One was getting around the solitary rider still ahead of him. The other was the whoop-de-dos.

In motocross a whoop-de-do is a stretch of bad bumps in the track. Even at a slow speed one's front wheel is going up while the back one is going down. This hazard turns every bike into a rodeo bronco.

A Sad Story

The lead rider prudently started to slow up for the bad stretch of track. Charlie knew that it was now or never. So he poured on the pedal power, charging into the whoop-de-dos as fast as he could make the wheels go around.

This was not smart, but Charlie was getting desperate. He was not the kind to settle for second place. He was already seeing himself saying "Thank you" to the judge who handed him his first-place trophy.

Charlie is our hero, and heroes should win. But it is only in books that this always happens. So Charlie, who had been riding his bike too fast into the rough ground, suddenly found the bike riding *him*.

At least he was a fighter. He scrambled up and remounted. He had some breath knocked out of him, but otherwise he was unhurt. His padded clothing and helmet protected him. The only thing hurt was his pride as he crossed the finish line, once again Tail-End Charlie.

Old Charlie consoled himself with the thought that he had really run the best race. Hadn't he come from behind to scare the pants off the front runner in that final stretch?

Actually, he had run a good race *part* of the time. But he would have run a better race—and perhaps a winning one—if he had used his brakes more instead of depending upon breaks. He lost a good chance when he messed up his start. Then he let himself get boxed in on the jump. Finally, he completely threw away the race by going recklessly into the whoop-de-dos.

There is no question that he was the fastest rider on the track that day. But Charlie had not learned that in motocross races are not won on speed alone.

Motocross is a thinking person's race, and a winner has to be thinking all the time. This does not mean that speed is not important. After all, it is only in little kiddies' picture books that the tortoise outruns the hare. But it does mean that in BMX, pure speed is not the answer. You have to get in there and work for victory.

2. Safety on the Track

It is easy to see why young people like BMX. It is exciting; it has variety; and it gives a boy or girl a chance to start racing at a much younger age than usual.

But parents like it too. The main reason is that it is safer than minibike and minicycle racing, the two main power-wheeled racing sports for young people. A minibike is a scooter-type vehicle powered by a lawn mower engine. Minicycles are scaled down motorcycles.

While it is possible to get hurt in BMX, bicycle motocross is the safest of all wheeled racing sports, with the possible exception of minibikes.

Thus many parents who are afraid for their children to race powered vehicles readily let them join BMX pedal-powered racing clubs.

It is normal for a sports group to claim that its sport is the safest thing going. In the case of BMX we do not have to listen to its fans give us a snow job. We can go to the one group that is least likely to gloss over BMX dangers. This group is made up of the people who sell insurance to race promoters. You can tell how dangerous they think a sport is by asking how much their premiums are. Insurance rates can change quickly, but right now a track can get full insurance coverage for one day's racing for about sixty dollars. This is insurance to protect the race promoters from liability. It is not insurance for the individual racer, although some tracks may carry this also. The low insurance rates show that the insurance agencies do not think there is much risk.

Waiver of Claims

To be honest about the matter, I must admit that these low insurance rates are based on two important points. One is the promoter's safety rules and his reputation for enforcing them. The other is that you—or your parent, if you are under eighteen—must sign a *waiver of claims*. This waiver says plainly that neither a track owner nor a promoter is responsible for anything that happens to you or your equipment.

If you sign such a waiver, why does the track need liability insurance anyway? This waiver *might* not be valid if the operators were grossly negligent—that is, if they were sloppy about track safety. This would be for the courts to decide. Also, the insurance protects the track from spectator claims, since they don't sign waivers.

Most waivers also obligate your parents to pay for any damage you cause to others. Thus if you—and I hope you won't—get mad because Johnnie beats you, and you kick out his bike spokes, your parents are stuck with the bill of replacing them. Or worse if you do worse damage.

Safety Points

Recklessness, poor equipment, and lack of safety gear are the three major sources of injury in BMX.

Reckless riding is a state of mind that a rider has to overcome. It is almost exclusively done by beginners. A seasoned rider has already learned that reckless riding is poor riding. Once in a while taking a chance may win a race, but most of the time recklessness leads to losses.

It can also lead to a rider's being thrown out of a race. Race promoters know that recklessness on the track causes injuries. And injuries mean increases in insurance and a black eye for the sport.

Recklessness also angers parents, who then object to their children's participating in the sport. But loudest of all the objectors are the riders themselves. You will find no admiration among them for a reckless rider. It is no fun to have pedaled your heart out to get a good chance to win and be spilled because a gung-ho idiot cuts too close in front of you, causing you and him to bite the dirt.

Another type of reckless riding is trying to blast your way through too small a hole between two leading riders. Still another is trying to pass on the inside when there is not enough clearance between you and the inside rider.

I saw this happen once. A determined rider found himself boxed in on a left turn. He thought he saw an opening on the inside between the inside rider and the bales of hay being used to mark the track.

I don't recall the rider's name, but it might have been Charlie. Old Charlie is the type.

Now there might have been room to pass when Charlie first spotted what he thought was an open door to victory. But passing on the inside is a poor gimmick at best and should be avoided. The hole—if there really was one—had narrowed down by the time Charlie pedal powered his way into it.

He banged into the other rider, who was knocked to the side, just enough to interfere with the rider coming up on his right. This brought three riders down in the dirt.

Then a fourth, following too closely, was unable to turn fast enough to avoid piling on top of a downed cycle. Charlie, scrambling to get off the course, narrowly missed being hit in the seat of his pants by an oncoming cycle. This was unfortunate, the spectators thought, for if ever anyone needed a boot in the seat, it was Old Charlie.

Cutoffs

Cutting another rider off is a reckless stunt to be avoided. Cutoffs can be done deliberately to try to prevent a rider from passing you. Or they can be just plain wild riding, done by swinging back in front of a cycle you have passed before there is sufficient clearance.

Either way, a rider who cuts off other riders should be ruled off the track. He is a menace to himself and others, as well as a liability to the entire sport.

There are no set rules in BMX like those in Y-AMA (Youth Division of the American Motorcycle Association), which governs sportsmanship in junior motorcycle racing. But track officials would do well to adopt the Y-AMA system as much as possible. Y-AMA requires a rider to be two full lengths in front of another rider before cutting in front of him.

This is for motorcycle racing, of course. Bicycles do not travel as fast as motorcycles, so you do not have to be as far ahead of the other rider as in the motor sport. But it is still a good idea to be at least two lengths in front if you can.

In any sport, interfering with another contestant is not legal. So if you cut in too closely in front of someone you are passing and he runs into you, it is your fault. Such a bump could put you both on the ground and out of the race. But even if you do manage to go on and win, you could be disqualified for interfering and for unsafe riding. So it is best to observe the two length rule and be safer, even if the local rules do not require it.

Flags and Flagmen

Next to the riders, the most important people at any race are the flagmen. They are the policemen who keep things running and the riders in order. They are stationed around the track and have flags that spell out important messages or orders.

Flagmen are used in motor sports because the loud engines of racing cars and motorcycles drown out orders or warnings. This noise, of course, is missing in motocross racing, but the flags and flagmen have been retained to give the flavor of motor sports to BMX. Also, flags can be flashed more quickly and are less easily misunderstood than shouted emergency commands.

Five different-colored flags are used in motor sports. Each tells its own story.

A sideline flagman waves his green flag to let the starter know that the track is clear and he can start the race.

The GREEN flag is used by a flagman to start a race. He waves the flag in the air several times and then brings it down sharply to signal riders to take off.

As will be discussed later, this is not the best way to start. Some tracks do not have mechanical starting gates and still use flag starts.

The WHITE flag is seldom used in BMX because it is the signal to riders that only one lap is left to go. BMX races rarely have more than one lap, although very occasionally for older riders a race may run two-lap motos. Even then you do not need a flagman to tell you how much you have left to do.

The YELLOW flag is one you must pay particular attention to. This is a warning that there is danger on the track. A yellow flag does not require you to stop, but you should slow down and watch for trouble.

This flag is not used much in BMX racing. It is usually used to signal spills on the track. Since you are on a bicycle, and are going around only one lap, you are not likely to run into any danger from spills. Besides, if someone falls he is usually so close to you that there is no time for the flagman to wave a signal anyway.

There are occasions, however, when a yellow flag can be used in BMX. One of these is when a large number of riders is going to race in one day. Then race officials may decide to hurry things up by starting groups more closely behind each other. This means that they might start the second wave of riders when the first is only halfway around the track.

In a case like this, if there is a pileup around a corner or after a jump, a yellow warning to the riders coming up in the second start would save them from running over the spilled riders.

A RED flag means STOP! When you see the crimson flash, you go no farther and return to the starting line.

This does not necessariy mean that there is danger on the track, although it could. It may mean that there has been a false start and the starter is calling you back to try again. This can happen when there is a foul and someone jumps the green flag on the start.

And finally there is the flag everyone is watching for. This is the BLACK-AND-WHITE-checkered flag. It means that the race is over. The first rider to get the checkered flag is the winner of the moto.

Safety Minded

All rules and flags have been set up to help keep the sport safe. But the rules are worthless if the rider is not safety minded himself. The rules force you to protect yourself with safety gear, but this is not enough. You must be safety minded and learn how to take care of yourself.

One of the best ways to take care of yourself is to learn how to fall. My friend Old Charlie does not think this is something one needs to learn. As he raced, he would find himself falling—without having to learn how! It just happened—and happened more often than is proper for a budding hot-shoe rider, or so he thought.

He missed the point. Anybody who rides a two-wheeled racing vehicle is going to fall. Plowing up dirt is part of the sport. What you must learn is how to protect yourself in a fall. If you can do this, you will not only save yourself many painful bruises, but will sometimes recover fast enough to get back in the race.

Proper Clothing

The first step in gentling your bounces on the ground is to cushion the shock with proper clothing. Racers who like to show their muscles by riding in T-shirts and shorts are going to have those muscles sandpapered away after they slide across the ground a few times.

A well-run track will not permit riders to run unless dressed in protective gear, but there are sandlot tracks where dress is not properly policed. Some of the better tracks and meets do permit short sleeves, provided the rider wears elbow protectors.

Elbow guards are important safety devices. Also note the foam padding on the crossbar between the handlebars.

A well-dressed BMX rider will wear a helmet, face protector, long—preferably padded—pants, long-sleeved shirt of heavy material, elbow and knee protectors, gloves, high-top shoes, and chest protector with shoulder pads.

Few riders go all the way with this safety equipment, although I recommend that they do. In any event, a helmet, goggles, gloves, and knee and elbow protectors are absolutely essential.

Helmets

Any injury is painful and dangerous, but a head injury can be the most dangerous of all. This makes the helmet your single most important piece of safety gear. It is also the one you want never to skimp on. Get a good one. Some of the inexpensive helmets crack too easily when they take a hard jolt.

It is true that a BMX rider does not take as hard a fall as a motorcycle rider, but even so it is poor economy to buy a cheap helmet. You can be thrown pretty hard in BMX, or worse yet, be hit by an oncoming cycle if you slip and fall.

Your helmet should fit. It isn't protecting you if your head rattles around inside it. The padding should be comfortable, but not too soft.

You might think that the softer the padding, the better for your head if you get banged, but this is just not so. If the padding is too soft, it compresses too quickly when the helmet is struck hard. A padding that is more firm will compress more slowly. This helps absorb the shock. Of course, this does not mean that the padding should be as hard as the helmet shell. It has to be soft, but not too soft.

Types of Helmets

There are two basic types of helmets. The way they are named is confusing, since one is called the "full-cover-age helmet" and the other is the "full-face helmet." This sounds a lot like saying the same thing in two different ways, but there is quite a difference between the two helmets.

The full-coverage helmet is open in front. It comes low over the forehead and down the sides of the face, but the front of the face, including the chin and neck, is exposed. There is no mouth protection and you must wear a face guard, also called a mouth guard, if you really want to be safe. This is a plastic cup that protects nose, mouth and chin. You attach it to sides of the helmet with elastic straps.

The full-face helmet is a "skull bucket." It fits completely over the head. There is an opening for the eyes. This type of helmet is heavier and some say it is less comfortable to wear. The smaller opening in front means that you cannot see as well. There are racers who will tell you that a rider does not need to see anything except the track in front of him. Others like to keep an eye on the competition. They claim that in the full-face helmet you have to turn your head too far to see to the side and back.

Some also claim that the full-face helmet is less safe.

This is a full coverage helmet, complete with a plastic mask to protect the rider's mouth and teeth.

This is because it might scrape against the chin or nose if it got knocked off in a fall. This argument originated with motorcycle riders, who fall at much higher speeds than bicycle riders.

So it has never been determined which of the two types is better.

Helmet Inspection

You don't buy a helmet and then forget about it. A helmet has to be taken care of, and should be inspected after every race to see that it can still do the job.

Helmets are made of either plastic or fiberglass. Banging a helmet around—either through hard spills or by careless handling—can cause cracks that weaken it. Then the next time you take a hard bounce, the helmet could break. This is especially true of some cheap models.

Helmets must be carefully inspected after every spill. Due to the way the helmet curves, impact force can be transmitted to other parts of the helmet when it is struck hard. This can cause breaks in parts of the helmet other than just where it struck the ground.

In addition, the mold that was used to make the helmet may have been imperfect, leaving weakened places in it. These can give way under light banging.

Any type of break in a helmet is dangerous. A small hairline crack that you might think is too small to worry about weakens the helmet. This could cause it to fail the next time you spill.

Inspecting the Helmet Padding

When inspecting your helmet pay close attention to the inside padding. This is especially important when the helmet starts to get old. If the padding becomes hard or compressed, it will no longer do its job. It will not absorb the jolt when your head hits the ground.

Some helmets are made with the padding cemented inside. Others have removable padding. A third type of padding is made for some motorcycle racing helmets. It is rigid and collapses when hit with a jolt. It does not spring back and has to be replaced after each shock.

Replacing Helmets

There is a lot of argument about when helmets should be replaced. Some manufacturers recommend you dump the old helmet and get a new one every two or three years. They argue that time and wear weaken the helmet material.

These people, of course, are trying to sell more helmets. They may be right, but I know of no tests that have been made to see how helmets stand up under normal wear. Helmet manufacturers have machines that bang helmet samples against hard surfaces as part of their design work and quality control. But even if they recalled a batch of helmets after three years to study material fatigue, I am not sure how much good this would do. There would be no way of determining how much rough treatment the helmet has gone through.

The treatment of a helmet is probably more important than its age.

About Visors

Visors on helmets have become popular in the last few years. Visors are not required safety items in BMX racing, but they are very helpful. They keep the sun out of your eyes. If you are wearing a plastic face shield or goggles, the visor helps keep the sun from reflecting off them.

Face Shields

Face shields are also not required items at this time, but they should be. Full-face plastic shields that snap on the helmet and protect the whole face afford the best protection. If they are not used, then a rider should certainly use a mouth guard, as explained under *Types of Helmets.*

Goggles, which are necessary in motorcycle racing, are rarely worn in BMX. But if one does not have a face shield, it is not a bad idea to use goggles. BMX tracks are dusty, even though they are usually wetted down several times during a race session. Wheels kick up clods that sometimes hit the faces of riders in the back. And if there are mud bogs, it is hard to keep the goo from hitting your face. Goggles and face plates can be very helpful then.

It is important to remember that poor-quality goggles, shields, and mouth guards are worse than none at all. Glass can shatter or be broken by rocks thrown back by spinning wheels. Be sure that whatever you buy is shatterproof.

The same thing is true if you wear glasses. If you normally wear eyeglasses, you should race in them. You certainly need clear vision. But be sure that you wear safety glasses that have shatterproof lenses. Face shields are especially important for people who wear glasses.

Body Protection

In BMX you do not need the heavy leathers motorcycle racers wear. Heavy jeans, worn with knee and elbow protectors, work well enough.

The popularity of BMX has started manufacturers turning out some pretty fancy duds for our sport. Some of their matched pants and jerseys really make a rider stand out from the pack. Their bright reds, yellows, blues, oranges, and greens are eye-catchers. In addition to their looks, they are—of course—built for safety. You see this kind of clothing at big nationals more than at small local tracks.

The best BMX pants are made of top-quality heavy-duty nylon. They have padded leather-covered knees, hip pads, and padded shin guards. They may be obtained in various color combinations to fit team colors.

Prices in 1979 run close to fifty dollars for the smaller sizes. Bigger riders will pay five to seven dollars in most cases.

BMX Jerseys and Shoes

Jerseys come in either 100-percent nylon or half nylon, half acrylic fibers. They come in rainbow colors, and some companies will stencil your name on them for you. Be sure the jersey you select has padded elbows. This will save you having to add elbow guards.

At a BMX nationals race, you will see riders wearing pretty fancy clothing. This is a ten-year-old expert class of riders.

One manufacturer advertises his BMX shoes as having "fully padded collar and tongue, flared outsole for extra traction with wrap-up toe and heel. Heavy-duty yellow nylon upper with split black leather toe, heel, and sides." Sounds neat! Riders who wear them say they are comfortable and give good support. Prices, depending upon the size, are in the twenty-five-dollar-and-up class.

Then you top off your costume with BMX gloves—orange with white-and-black backing, and reinforced on the back to take bumps.

The result is as classy a dude as you will see on the track.

It's Costly

Dressing up in BMX style is costly, but fortunately a pair of jeans and a helmet can get you through if you don't have the money for fancy duds.

But if you do buy them, get good quality. Cheap stuff falls apart quickly. A couple of spills and you'll be sewing patches on your seat.

Price is not necessarily an indication of quality. Some rip-off artists deliberately overprice their junk to con suckers into thinking they are getting the best. Fortunately, this kind of sharpster doesn't last long. Word gets around that he is peddling junk and his business falls off. BMX riders are a friendly bunch of Joes. Ask around the track. Riders who have been stuck with junk, either clothing or riding equipment, will tell you what to avoid.

Inside the Suit

Fancy clothes of the best quality will not get you a trophy unless what is in the suit is top quality also. Physical fitness is the first requirement for winning in any kind of sport.

This means all-over fitness. Strong legs are a basic requirement. But legs are fed by blood pumped by a heart that depends on strong lungs. Strength in arms and shoulders is needed for steering and for picking up and pushing down the front of the bike during jumps.

A regular routine of calisthenics—concentrating on deep knee bends, and trunk, arm, and shoulder exercises—should be used along with a daily hard schedule of bike riding. Some champions never ride in a car if they can help it. With them it is biking all the way.

A word of caution, however. A racing bike should be kept for racing. Because the riders try to make their bikes as light as possible, many racing bikes are not street legal—that is, legally acceptable for street use. Also, remember that you can get a traffic citation for speeding on a bicycle, just as you can for speeding in a car. Be careful where you practice racing.

Taking a Tumble

In any kind of two-wheel-vehicle racing, it is not a question of *if* you fall, but *when* you fall and *how*. You are going to spill many times.

No spill is ever pleasant. Sometimes it can be downright dangerous. You can break a leg, an arm, or even your neck. But you can also do that—and a legion of people have—right at home in the bathtub. No one has suggested that we give up bathing just because so many accidents happen in the bathroom. Nor should we have to give up sports.

And, as sports go, BMX is one of the safest. Proper observance of the rules, good safety gear, and good bikes (which we will talk about later) help to make it that way. Most books, articles in magazines, and BMX instruction by groups or individuals stress these three vital things.

But there is something else you can do that instructors do not talk about as much as they should. You can learn how to fall properly.

In talking about padded pants, elbow guards, and other protective materials, it would appear that we have been talking about how to take care of yourself in a fall. This is true. These items cushion the fall, and save bruises and maybe broken limbs or scrambled brains. But you can make a fall still easier and *get back into the race faster* if you learn to fall properly.

I know, Old Charlie and a lot of other hot shoes will tell you that there is no such thing as a proper way to fall. Any fall is improper and shouldn't happen.

That is correct, but the pedaler has never yet shown up who can avoid spills forever. To find out how to fall, our best bet is to watch a group that takes falls as part of their business. They call themselves tumblers.

Tumbling Tricks

Have you ever watched a circus clown take a pratfall? Or seen a cowboy shot from the saddle in a movie? These people and others like them have been trained to fall. They are tumblers. They can wham their bodies against the floor or ground and come up on their feet after a fall that would leave some of us yelling for a doctor to put our pieces back together again.

These clowns and stunt men have no real secrets. They use the basic tricks taught in gymnastic and tumbling classes, where the first thing you learn is how to fall.

We do not have the space here to go into the intricate art of tumbling. That takes a full book in itself. But I would like to give a few examples.

One type of fall is the shoulder roll. In this tumble, the stunt man falls forward. He uses his arms to break his fall. At the same time he throws his right shoulder down and forward so that he rolls over on this shoulder.

He then flexes his knees and rolls across his back from the right to the left shoulder. If his knees were bent correctly, this causes him to roll right over onto his knee. The continuation of the roll will bring the other knee to the ground. The force left from the roll gives his body a lift. This helps bring the tumbler to his feet again.

A fall does not necessarily mean a lost race. Here a rider, going too fast into a turn, bites the dirt. But he is not the quitting kind.

This may sound a bit complicated in the telling, but it is easily learned. It is standard training for football players.

The Forward Roll

Another tumbling trick is the forward roll. In this one the tumbler breaks his fall with his hands as in the shoulder roll. Then he tucks his head and rolls forward in a somersault. The forward push of his body helps him lift back on his feet.

The second picture shows how he bounced up and is back in the race before the moto's Tail-end Charlie can pass him by.

In all of these rolls, the secret of an easy fall is in using the body as a spring to reduce and absorb some of the shock of falling.

To demonstrate this to yourself, stand on a chair and jump *stiff-legged* to the floor. You can feel the shock jar up your legs. Now repeat the jump, but this time *flex your knees.* The "give" in your legs, caused by the spring action of your knees, absorbs part of the shock. And you get an easier landing.

It is the same when you use your arms, legs, or shoulder to break a fall. If you hit the ground stiffly, you are going to transmit shock right up into your body. You might even break an arm. But if the arm is flexed properly, it acts as a spring, protecting itself and your body from shock.

More Than Protection
The ability to fall without getting the wind knocked out of you and the ability to recover quickly will benefit your racing a great deal. As a beginner, you are on the same level with the rest of the riders in your race. They are beginners too. They make mistakes, get caught in jam-ups, and fall. If you can recover quickly enough, it is quite possible to get back into the race.

You may not win, but you can make a credible showing, which is better than tagging along fighting Charlie for tail-end position. I've seen crowds give as good a hand to a never-say-die who fought himself back into a pretty good position as they did to the winner. The sports world loves a fighter.

Therefore, it is not a bad idea to learn a little something about tumbling. You should learn in a class. Instructors recommend that beginners in gymnastics never practice without a "spotter" to check them out. There is no place for self-instruction here. Get good advice and follow it.

3. BMX Tracks

BMX is the newest thing in bicycle racing, but cycle racing itself will be three hundred years old come 1990. It was in 1690 that a Frenchman put wheels on each end of a pole. He straddled the pole, pushed off with his feet, and tried to ride it down a hill. There were no brakes, no way to steer. He just rolled and hoped for the best.

He got a bumpy ride and a spill at the end. But his idea caught on. Soon other young men joined him, racing each other to see who could get the farthest downhill before being thrown off. Bumps, bruises, and broken limbs were all part of the fun.

This thing, the prototype of the bicycle, was called a *celerifère*. It was around for 126 years before Baron Karl von Drais put a pivoting front wheel and handlebars on it. Grateful *celerifère* fans were so pleased that they re-named it the *draisienne* in honor of the inventor. Steering permitted them to go farther without so many falls.

English youth took up the draisienne, but could not pronounce the name. So they just called it the *bone-shaker*. The name fit. These English lads not only rode the contraption downhill, but pushed themselves along the street, using their legs like a scooter. The cobblestone streets and lack of suspension made for a very rough ride. Jokers of the day said that draisienne fans were so lazy they had to sit down when they walked.

Then in 1870 James Starley put pedals on the boneshaker. There were no gears. So he made the front wheel very large and the back wheel small. The pedals were attached directly to the large front wheel. Thus one revolution of the pedals carried the rider quite a distance.

The high front wheel made these pioneer bicycles dangerous to ride. This did not stop the young sportsmen of the day. Bicycling became a popular fad. Clubs were formed and bicycle racing got started.

Then in 1880 the chain-and-sprocket drive was invented. It reduced the dangerous front wheel on bicycles, bringing about what was then called the "safety bike." Interest in bicycle racing increased.

Bicycle racing has remained popular in Europe, but in the United States interest in it gave way to motorcycle and automobile racing as these new machines were introduced.

In time, motorcycle racing became less popular in this country. About the only place one could see motorcycle racing was at fairs each year. These races were run mainly by professional riders who traveled the fair circuit.

The renewed boom in two-wheel racing came after World War II, when Honda invaded the American motorcycle market with good, relatively low-priced cycles.

Then the invention of motorcycle motocross gave cycle racing a new life, producing the fastest-growing new sport in this country.

A Place to Ride

Today BMX is booming as rapidly as motorcycle motocross did a few years ago. It would be even further along if there were more places for eager riders to race.

Another thing that has slowed BMX down is that at first bikes were not strong enough for the beating BMX gives them. This is changing now, because manufacturers are building bicycles designed for BMX riding.

In this sport every part of the cycle comes under heavy pounding. This requires strength and special construction. But if a manufacturer beefed up a cycle as much as he should for this kind of heavy riding, the thing would be so heavy that it would be useless for racing. It would be like a workhorse instead of a racehorse.

The challenge in building BMX cycles is to achieve strength with lightness. This is very difficult to do, but it must be done, because the lighter a cycle is, the faster it will go.

But before going into the details of what a good BMX cycle should be, we should first take a look at a BMX track. This will show us why we need a bike that can take punishment as well as float lightly over man-made hazards.

The BMX Track

No two BMX tracks are ever exactly alike. The reason for this is that the available land will determine the

This pretty track is the BMX layout at the Los Angeles Regional Park at La Mirada, California. It is a fast downhill course.

character of the track. If the track designer has a downhill slope to work with, he can build a faster track. In this case the turns should be banked higher so riders can take turns at this higher speed.

If the land is flat, then a starting mound will probably be provided to get riders away from the line faster. The shape of the parcel of land available will then determine where the turns and jumps or other hazards are placed. Thus on one track you may have a turn right after the start, while at another there may be a straightaway.

If the land is small and square, then there will be more and tighter turns in order to tuck everything into the smaller space.

Sometimes there are mud and sand, but a lot of tracks are dropping these hazards now, but this is not true motocross.

However, although the shape and placement of the hazards vary, you will find that all BMX tracks have certain things in common. All have right and left turns, including both banked and flat corners. All have jumps of various heights, straightaways, and whoop-de-dos (rough areas).

The Starting Line

The starting line is usually on a mound, as we have mentioned before. However, the *way* the races are started can be quite different at one track from another. Also, the number of riders who can race at one time may be different. If lack of land has forced a narrow track, then fewer riders can run in each moto. On some tracks as many as twelve riders can start at once. At others the number who can start at one time may be as few as six. For safety's sake, it is very important that each rider have enough space to prevent bumping those on either side.

Mechanical Gates

The best way to start a race is with a mechanical gate. This may be made of wood, pipe, or even heavy mesh

Some starting lines are built on mounds. Here the entrants are coming from the staging area to line up behind the plywood gate. The gate will flop down when the race starts.

fencing wire. It is hinged to a facing set in the ground. When raised and locked in place, the mechanical gate makes a fence that keeps riders from pushing across the line or starting too early.

The gate falls when the starter pushes a lever. The riders roll over it and down the starting mound for a fast, fair start. Such a gate prevents fouls.

Rubber-Band Starts

A track that doesn't have the money to put in a mechanical starting gate may use a rubber-band start instead.

This start is just what the name implies: A length of rubber tubing is stretched across the starting line in front of the racers. When this is dropped, they are off.

Why a rubber band instead of string or rope? Because eager entrants keep pushing against it. They would continually be breaking a light cord and might get rope burns or cut themselves.

A rubber-band start cannot control a line of riders as well as a mechanical gate can, but it is the fastest way to make mass starts. Where there are a lot of riders, there is no better way to get them on the track quickly.

In a motorcycle grand prix I once saw, the starters put five hundred riders on the track, one wave right behind the other, in nine minutes flat. In this start the cycles were lined up fifteen abreast in rows stretching down the track. One rubber band was stretched in front of the first line and another in front of the second line. As soon as the first band was snapped up to start that line, it was brought over the heads of the second line and dropped in front of the third line.

None of the lines moved up to start. They started from their original positions. This extra distance was figured into their running times so that it was fair to all.

Flag Starts

Many small tracks still use flagmen for starts. Flag starts cause more trouble than rubber-band or gate starts. There is nothing here but the watchful eye of the starter to keep eager riders from trying to inch a bit ahead of the others.

The extra inch or so that one can get ahead of the others may not really make any difference, but a lot of riders think it does. And they crowd the line for all they are worth.

Even worse, they try to jump the flag, getting away ahead of the others. It definitely helps to leave the starting line first, for that way a rider can avoid getting hemmed in on the first turn.

There is also a psychological advantage to being first off the line. A blistering takeoff can take the heart out of your competition. That is, it can scare some of them. But there is always a bullheaded joker in the crowd who won't let you "psych" him. All you can do with that kind of joker is to get in there and flat outrace him.

Meeting Competition

In a horse race a jockey may hold his mount back. He lets the others tire their horses out. Then he plies the whip and starts moving up to take the lead. But BMX is not a horse race—despite the fact that you often feel you are racing with donkeys. You have less than one minute to get from start to finish. That leaves no time for fooling around. One of the secrets of BMX is to get in front and *stay there*—if you can.

Riders know this. So there is considerable jockeying around to get any advantage that may be had. This causes some false starts. An overeager rider will hit his pedals before the flag comes down. This rarely works, for the flagman is watching for this sort of thing.

Then everybody gets the red flag. They are recalled to

the starting line for another start. If the same person continues to foul, he might be disqualified.

Outsmarting the Flagman

So you can't ignore the flagman and start when you please. But you *can* try to outsmart him. This is not easy. Flagmen are smart themselves. But it can be done.

What you want to do here is to actually jump the flag. But you have to do it in a legal way. You can do it the way a lot of people play poker. That is, you can learn to "read" the flagman. After all, he is human too. He often gives away his intentions by the way he acts. He does the same thing so often that he falls into a groove or pattern. This can give a smart rider a clue to what the flagman is going to do before he does it.

The theory behind this is that your brain has to realize that something is happening before it can send a message for your muscles to act. If you see a fist coming at your face, your brain has to yell at your muscles, "duck!" before they contract to move you out of danger. After the brain realizes that there is danger, the time it takes before the muscles act is called "reaction time." If you can tell a split second before he does it what the flagman is going to do, then you can be prepared and can cut your own reaction time. This will get you off the line quicker.

Study the Flagman

Flagmen often give themselves away unconsciously. One may raise himself on his toes just before he brings the flag down to start. Another may have a different oddity. If you study each flagman carefully, you can often discover some little mannerism that gives away his intentions.

I know one motorcycle motocross rider who leaves his bike with a friend in the staging area. He gets out where he can watch the flagman start the motos before his own. He claims he can often pick up things that help him get a faster start.

The Track Itself

As we noted before, tracks differ. They may be arranged differently. Some may be harder than others. Some may twist more. But they all have to include the following or you are not on a real motocross course.

Straightaways and Turns

From the starting line there is a straightaway. This is to give you a good fast start to the first turn. The turn (corner) may be flat, which means that it is not banked at all. This type of corner is difficult to make if the turn is sharp. You must slow down for it. That often causes a pileup, since those following too closely behind the front-runners have to slow as those in front put on the brakes.

The turn may also be banked. This permits you to take it at a much faster speed. Later we will talk about how to corner properly. Right now, the main point is to get a clear idea of what the track is like.

Jumps

After the first turn you may face your first jump. There are three types of jumps. One is the downhill jump. That means that you land at a lower spot than you took off from. An uphill jump is one where you land on higher ground than the place you left. A horizontal jump is a mound in the track, and you land at the same level you started from.

Banked Turns

After the jump there will be another straightaway that leads you into another corner. If the first corner was

In a downhill jump, the rider lands at a lower level than he took off from. On most tracks the front rider would be required to wear either a long sleeve shirt or elbow pads.

flat, the second one will be banked, so you can take it faster.

In a regular banked turn the track is lower on the inside of the track than on the outside. The high outside helps balance centrifugal force—the force that tends to push you outward when you go around a corner at a fast speed.

But just to throw in a surprise, some track designers may put in an *off-camber corner*. This is where the slope of the turn has a high inside and a low outside. You see this most often in desert or cross-country racing, but it has been known to pop up on BMX tracks. It can be quite a surprise if you have never ridden one.

When you come out of a turn, there will always be a short straight to let you get ready for what comes next. You can't relax, however, for BMX courses are all crowded. You must keep alert at all times. On a well-designed course each turn and jump will be different in some way from the one that you went over last. If the last jump was a horizontal one, then this one may be a downhiller. If the last turn was a wide curve, then the next one may be a hairpin turn that taxes your ability to keep upright.

Mud and Sand

You may also find yourself in the middle of a mudhole. Mud is unpleasant to ride through and plain miserable to fall in. It is very hard on your cycle, for it gets into all the moving parts.

Why do tracks include the stuff? Well, mud is a part of

motocross. Spectators love it. For the riders, mud on a race track can be quite tricky. It takes a special technique to ride it swiftly. The only thing good about it from a rider's standpoint is that if you fall, the stuff is soft.

After the mud bath, you may hit a stretch of sand. If the track is being used for both very small and larger riders, neither the sand nor the mud will be too deep. But if a separate track is set up for the older teens, the sand—as well as the mud before it—may be quite deep.

Whoop-de-dos

After the sand there may be another turn and then, just before you go into the final stretch, you'll have to bump your way through the rough whoop-de-dos. If you get through these, you have just a short straightaway before the checkered flag falls for you.

Indoor Tracks

Not all BMX tracks are out in the dirt. Indoor tracks are beginning to appear. Beginners will generally do better on outdoor tracks. Dirt is softer than wood or concrete, although indoor tracks generally soften their wooden jumps with carpeting. A sensible promoter will sprinkle resin on *indoor* turns to give tires a better grip.

In California they have staged BMX races that are half outdoor races. One example is the coliseum races put on under the joint sponsorship of Mongoose (BMX Products, Inc.) and NBA (National Bicycle Association, a BMX sanctioning group).

One of these coliseum races was held recently in the Los Angeles Coliseum at halftime during a football game. Some jumps and course markers were hastily moved onto the field. The BMX track was arranged in the form of the letter M. One portable wooden jump—the biggest one—was placed in the center of the field on the fifty-yard line. Three other jumps were placed on the west end of the field. Then seventy riders showed the audience of fifty thousand what BMX was all about.

The men who set up the course did a splendid job of moving quickly on and off the track. It was a good show

Whoop-de-dos are a stretch of very rough ground. Here a pack of twelve-year-old riders at an NBA nationals meet tackle one of these spill-makers.

and an excellent advertisement of BMX for a lot of people who would never have bothered to see a race otherwise. Of course, you can't satisfy everyone. I heard one spectator grouse, "If they had to have a halftime show, I'd rather have seen the Dallas Cowgirls." Perhaps there were others who would have preferred pretty girls with pretty legs strutting around at the half, but they obviously are not sports lovers.

4. The Motocross Bicycle

BMX pioneers quickly found out that their regular bicycles were not good enough for motocross. Frames cracked. Wheels broke. Gearing proved inadequate. Pedals were slippery. And the whole cycle was too heavy.

Like every sport, BMX needed equipment that had been designed for it. Fortunately, the rapid growth of BMX aroused manufacturers' interest. Now BMX special equipment is flooding the market. You can buy BMX cycles, stronger forks, mag wheels, hubs that are almost frictionless, and other specialties.

Boys and girls use the same bikes. The lack of a top brace on regular girls' bikes weakens them too much for motocross.

Have You Learned to Ride?

If you are ready to begin, you should already have learned to ride a bicycle. This may sound like a silly statement, but you will find riders who get their first bikes and want to start BMX before they get the training wheels off their cycles. I applaud their enthusiasm, but not their lack of good sense. You should not attempt to race until you have learned to ride well. Racing is postgraduate riding.

In addition to learning to ride, you should learn all you can about bicycles in general. This includes how to take care of them. You should also learn the names of the different parts of a bicycle. Then you will understand when someone speaks of the top tube or the down tube or the dropouts, and so on.

Unfortunately not everyone does this. So let us begin our discussion of the BMX cycle by reviewing the parts of a cycle frame. We begin with the frame because it is the foundation of the cycle—the basic element a manufacturer starts with in building your racing machine.

The Frame

The frame of a bicycle is made of tubing. The tubing is welded together to make three triangles, which are joined.

In the center, the welded triangles of tubing have a common leg, the center post called the *seat tube*. The bottom of the seat tube is welded to the *crank hanger*. The crank is the curved piece of metal that the pedals attach to. The top of the seat tube rises above the top of the frame to end in the *seat tube mast*. This is what your *seat post clamp* is attached to.

The seat tube is one leg of the *front triangle*. From it, two tubes run forward and are welded to the *steering head* to form the full front triangle. The steering head is where the *forks* for your front wheel fit and connect to the handlebars.

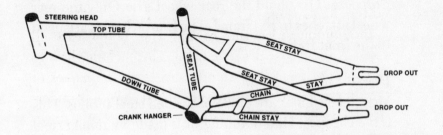

A bicycle frame is made up of tubing that has been welded together to make three triangles.

The tube running from the seat tube mast to the steering head is the *top tube,* in bicycle language. The other bracing tube is the bottom tube, but you don't call it that. It is the *down tube.* It connects the steering head and the crank hanger.

Two additional triangles of tubing make up the back part of the frame. The seat tube acts as one leg of these two triangles as well. The two rear triangles are identical, and form the cage that the rear wheel fits into. The top tube in the front triangle is straight, but the top members of the rear triangles are bent out so the wheel can fit between them. These top tubes are called the *seat stays.* The two bottom members that make up the rear triangles are the *chain stays.* Just back of the seat tube two short crossbars give support and strength.

At the back end of each of the rear triangles, the point where the seat stay and chain stay meet has been welded to a piece of slotted metal. These slots are the *dropouts*. They hold the rear wheel axle. Only the rear wheel attaches to the frame. The front wheel is attached to the front forks.

How a Frame Is Made

Most bike frames are made of welded steel tubing. This is the cheapest kind of tubing. It is made by rolling steel into a tube and welding the seam.

A better frame is made of seamless tubing that has been hardened by alloys. Alloys are combinations of two or more metals for a specific purpose; in this case small amounts of metal are added to the steel to make it harder. Seamless alloy frames are stronger and lighter, and will "give" more before breaking.

The seam in welded steel tubing weakens the tube. This is because of the high temperature needed to melt the metal in welding. The heat causes a change in the carbon steel.

Also, it is easy to get defects in weld seams. You may have read how X rays showed many defects in the Alaskan pipeline welds. This same thing can happen in bike weld joints. A weld can be weakened by blowholes caused by gas bubbles trapped in the melted steel. Poor penetration, meaning the heat did not melt the metal deeply enough for a solid join, is another weld fault. And so on, through several defects that can make a weak weld.

Many of these welding defects will not cause much trouble with an ordinary street bike. But BMX is not ordinary riding. It is the most punishing use of a bicycle there is.

Some bicycle joints are *brazed* instead of welded. The difference is that in welding, the edges of the two pieces to be joined are melted and the metal flows together to make the joint. Filler—metal rods—is melted with the metal to fill up space where needed.

In brazing, the metal parts to be joined are heated. Then bronze-type metal rods are melted to flow between the two parts. The brazing metal acts as a "glue" to hold the parts together. Since brazing rod melts at a lower temperature than steel, brazing does not require as much heat. The base metal—the bicycle tubing itself—is never melted.

Welders claim that brazing makes a stronger frame than welding. The way metals are joined depends upon the type of metal used. Some hard metals cannot be welded without special and costly techniques.

Some bike frames are *double butted.* This means that the tubes are thicker at the ends. Such tubes are stronger than straight tubing, but they are also heavier.

Joint Welds

The frame takes more punishment than any other part of the cycle, including the rider. It has to support the wheels, forks, cranks, handlebars, seat, and rider. It is hammered by shock from every direction.

If there is a weak spot in the welds, this constant beating can cause a break that will put you out of the race in a hurry.

The weakest spots in the frame are the places where the tubes are welded together. Here is where cracks are most likely to begin. These cracks are rarely in the weld itself. They usually begin next to the weld, where the tube metal has been weakened by the heat of the welding torch.

You can sometimes spot these hairline cracks by examining the weld joints with a magnifying glass. If you notice even the tiniest crack, you should have it repaired before the bike is used again. This is especially true if you are going to do any hard jumping with the cycle. Once a crack starts, you are inviting trouble if you keep riding.

Weight Is the Problem

Making a strong bicycle is no problem. The trouble is that a strong cycle is often too heavy for racing.

The weight problem in a racing cycle is the same as the weight problem in automobile designing. Automakers are pushed by the government to make their cars lighter. This is because when you deal with energy there is nothing free. The more weight you have to move, the more energy it takes to move it.

Even the addition of five extra pounds to a car will require more energy to run it. With a car, the extra energy needed may be so small that you hardly notice it. But with a bike, an extra five pounds makes a tremendous difference. If a bike weighs—say—50 pounds, an addition of five pounds is a 10-percent weight increase. It will take more energy to move this extra weight—and

When you are riding like this, the weight of your cycle is an important factor in getting in front and staying there. The lighter the cycle, the less energy it takes to pedal it.

all this energy has to come from the rider's legs and lungs.

Licking the Weight Problem
So the lighter the cycle, the faster you can push it around the track. But you can't get something for nothing. You must give up some strength in order to have more speed. But if you give up strength in a BMX bicycle, you are going to beat the cycle to pieces in the hard world of the motocross track.

You can eliminate some weight by dropping the mud-guards, fenders, lights, reflectors and other devices that are required on a street-legal bicycle. This means that you cannot ride the cycle anywhere except on race-courses and private land.

Having eliminated all the extras you can, you next reduce weight further by turning to lightweight bicycle frames. They are being made now from special metal alloys originally developed for the aircraft industry. These alloys are lighter than ordinary steel and generally stronger. They are also more expensive.

Lightweight Frames

The average carbon-steel bicycle frame weighs 6 pounds or more. If the tubes are double butted, the frame may be a bit heavier.

The newer lightweight frames vary in weight. As this is written, one frame has been advertised as weighing 4 pounds, 3 ounces. It is made of molybdenum steel (moly), a high-strength, lightweight alloy. This frame is 33 inches long and provides a wheelbase of 37½ inches.

Another lightweight frame by an Arizona firm uses chrome moly to cut the weight to 3 pounds, 5 ounces. Another manufacturer is using hardened aluminum for frames. The hardening is done by heat treating. Then the welded joints are stress relieved. Stress is created in a weld joint when heat causes one part to harden to a different degree than surrounding parts. This causes pressures that lead to breaks.

Checking Them Out

There is a big difference between a manufacturer's claims and what some products really put out. Test articles you read in various magazines and papers help you make a decision on what to buy. But they are not the complete answer.

Recently the U.S. government brought charges against one of the nation's largest automobile manufacturers. The government charged that the company had been running its E.P.A. smog tests in specially-built engines. In the same manner, we do not always know what has been done to some of the test cycles we read about. Magazines which run product test stories do the best they can, but we cannot always be sure that some smart company representative has not put one over on them.

Also, magazines depend upon advertising to live. The price you pay for a publication does not cover the cost of getting it out. No magazine is going to laud some turkey. The paper cannot stay in business that way. But at the same time, the publisher is not going to nitpick the products of his best advertiser.

Some years ago a letter was produced in a court trial. A publisher had sent a memorandum to his editors telling them if they could not say something good about the products of an advertiser, they were not to say anything.

The toughest shakedown a product can get is from Consumer Reports. This company buys its test products on the open market from various locations and then gives them a real beating to see how they stand up. When these people give a good report, you can bet on it.

Ask the Man Who Owns One

Some years ago a big car manufacturer based an ad campaign on the slogan "Ask the man who owns one!" This is good advice for BMX products as well.

However, do not let yourself be influenced too much by company-sponsored riders. Champs who ride on company teams are good, or the company would not have taken them on. But all too often these riders do not race the stock bikes that you will be buying. A lot of their bikes have been specially built at greater expense than any company can afford to put into its stock models.

Then why can't you put a little more money into your bike and join the national winners in the trophy line? You might be able to do it. But you have to learn first that the bike is only part of the winning team. The rider is the other part. To get into the winning class, you must first do a lot of racing in the little meets back home.

Forks and the Front End

There is not much you can do about the handlebars. Make sure the hand grips are tight and won't slip on you. Motocross handlebars also have a cross brace on them to add strength.

The forks, however, are a different matter. The forks consist of a rod that passes through the steering head and then splits into two legs for the front wheel to ride between. The wheel axle slips between two dropouts (slots) at the ends of the forks. The forks serve to support the front wheel and as part of the steering, for the top connects to the handlebars.

The problem with forks is the same as with the frame —we need strength with lightness. Tubular forks are made of tubes that have been pressed or welded together. Pressing means that the parts have been tightly forced together. Welded forks have the joints melted together. Welding makes a tighter joint than pressing, but pressed or welded forks of the tubular type can bend under the bang-bang pounding of a BMX course.

Forks that have been forged are better. Forging means that the red-hot metal is hammered into shape by a huge forging press. Forged forks are made in one piece, with no welded seams or press fittings to create possible weak points.

Cast forks can also be made in one piece, but are not as strong as forged forks. Cast parts are made by pouring liquid metal into a mold and letting it harden. Cast parts are usually brittle and break easily.

The need for lighter forks has brought some new items onto the market. Chrome moly, aluminum, and titanium are now being used. All of these metals are more expensive than the mild steel usually used.

Suspension

When ordinary forks are used, the only thing that absorbs road shock is the air in the tires. Pneumatic (airfilled) tires help, of course, but still a lot of bumps jar up into the frame and rider.

This has made a lot of riders wonder if suspension might help. Suspension means springs or shock absorbers. You can buy forks with shock absorbers and bikes with front and rear suspension.

There is disagreement about how much suspension helps racing. Some tracks don't care what you run, as long as you stick to the 20-inch wheel. Others put bikes with suspension into a separate class of their own. Suspension also adds a little extra weight.

Goosenecks

The gooseneck is the curved piece of metal that clamps to your handlebars and holds them to the forks. This is a very important piece of equipment, for if your handlebars come loose in a race, you are in a tough spot.

The gooseneck takes a lot of strain. In lifting over jumps, you are pulling up, then pressing down, on the handlebars. Also, in every fall the handlebars are jammed into the ground. All this puts more strain on the gooseneck.

For this reason the light, stamped-out goosenecks used on many street bikes are no good for racing. Stamped-out parts are punched out of cold metal by dies. Forged-steel goosenecks are better, but they are heavy. A good hot-forged gooseneck may weigh over a pound—which is one third as much as some forks.

The importance of goosenecks has spurred manufacturers to find ways to maintain strength while taking off some ounces. A new gooseneck called Tuf-Nek was introduced recently. It is said to weigh under a pound and to be strong enough to support 80,000 pounds of pressure.

Wheels

A complete wheel includes the rim, spokes, and hub. (We will talk about the tires a little later.)

The wheel is measured from the bottom to the top of the tire, and not from rim edge to rim edge. BMX racing has standardized on the 20-inch wheel. Standardization is necessary because there are so many age classes that races would be too long if another dozen classes had to be added to take care of different sizes of cycles.

The 20-inch standard seemed a good compromise between the bigger bikes older riders would prefer and the smaller bikes that younger riders must have. The general rule for bike height is that you be able to straddle the top tube and have your feet firmly on the ground.

The only exception to the 20-inch wheel is when some tracks let very young riders use smaller bikes. As professional BMX develops, we will probably see a professional class develop that will go to bigger wheels—say 26 inches. Larger wheels will increase possible danger, since the bigger the wheel the faster you can go. This means a harder bump when you fall.

The 20-incher is a good compromise and a reason BMX is one of the safer racing sports.

Rims

There are three types of rims. One is the solid rim. It is made by running a piece of solid metal through a forming machine that curves it into a dish shape to hold the tire in place. Then the formed metal is bent by another machine into a perfect circle. The ends are welded. This is the least strong of the various types of rims.

The second type is much like the first, except that the maker uses tubing instead of solid metal. The tubing is flattened in the manufacture. That means that the rim has a double thickness. Ordinarily it will be stronger than the solid rim, but it is also heavier. The wheel of a BMX cycle takes quite a beating. So even though we want to reduce weight as much as we can, the wheel is a poor place to do it.

The third type of rim is part of a one-piece wheel. This wheel is made of cast aluminum. Here the rim, spokes, and hub are molded of a single piece. The bearings are then added. In addition to being all in one piece with strong struts instead of wire spokes to join hub and rim, the cast wheel is heat-treated to increase its strength.

This is the strongest wheel you can buy, but it is also the heaviest and the most expensive.

Spokes

One of the great advantages of the cast wheel is that you can stop worrying about spokes. Spoked wheels keep you busy adjusting the wires. Adjusting is done by tightening or loosening a threaded nut called a nipple. Too much tightening can pull your wheel out of round. Not enough tightening can cause the wheel to warp.

It does not seem possible that a few wires between

the rim and hub could support the full weight of a rider and the cycle frame. But if properly tightened and adjusted, a spoked wheel can support much more weight than it will ever be called upon to do.

Cycle craftsmen speak of spoke placement as lacing. The standard 20-inch BMX wheel is usually laced with number 80 spokes. What this means is that the wire used for the spokes is .080 inches in diameter.

Often the question is asked, "Can I make the wheel strong by putting in larger spokes?"

It's possible to buy spokes up to number 200. But then you would have to rebore all the spoke holes in the rim and hub. This is quite a job. This is especially so in the hub, where the holes are close together. You can easily ruin a wheel by trying to rebore it. So if you need bigger spokes to make a wheel stronger, you are better off buying a wheel that has them.

Hub

The hub is where the spokes are attached to the center of the wheel, where it revolves around the axle. It also houses the wheel bearings. A rear wheel contains the back sprocket gear and may have a hub brake as well.

Tires

The regular bicycle tire is not satisfactory for BMX. You need "knobbies," which are tires with a special tread that digs into the dirt and really pushes you along. Two sizes are used on 20-inch wheels.

One is 20 × 1.75. This number means that the tire fits

a 20-inch wheel and is 1.75 inches in diameter. Some riders like a wider wheel because "it puts more rubber on the ground." This means that more tire tread presses against the ground, and therefore gives more traction. The wider tire is 20 × 2.175.

It is possible to get still larger tires. Some factory riders have experimented with putting small motorcycle tires on their rear wheels.

Unfortunately for BMX, this wider-tire gimmick does not work as it does for hot rodding. These wide tires do not fit between the regular bicycle forks and rear cage unless you modify the cycle construction.

Then you run into a weight problem that more than offsets the advantage wider tires provide in traction. The larger tire, wheel, and hub all add extra weight. When you are using leg power on the track, an extra five pounds is a heavy burden to overcome.

Knobby Tires

Knobbies, with their heavy tread, are intended only for dirt racing. Here the lugs dig into the soft ground and really shove you along. They also grip on turns and save you from spills and slides.

But knobbies are no good on a hard, smooth track. The lugs keep a lot of the tire from pressing on the ground. They do not let you transmit to the track all the power your churning legs are putting out. On a hard track you are better off with a tire that has a smaller tread.

Knobby tires have rubber lugs molded into the tread. On a soft dirt track, these knobs dig, giving better traction. Knobbies are less effective on hard tracks.

Smooth Tires

Hot-rodders like slick tires made of softer rubber that really grips the track. BMX riders who have been hot-rod fans often ask about using slicks on their bicycles. Slicks —that is, tires without tread designs cut in them—work well on a hard, straight course. But they are absolutely no good for turns. The bottoms of the tires are flat, not rounded like a normal bicycle tire. You need that tread on the sides to grip the ground when you lean over on turns.

Ordinarily you will use knobby tires for BMX racing.

There may be times when you can race on ordinary street tires, but not often.

I recently visited a track that was BMX in name only. It was really a dirt track laid out with right and left turns, not the usual oval course. It had a few jumps, but no whoop-de-dos, mud, or sand. The track was also packed down pretty hard. I saw a number of riders with knobby tires, but it appeared to me that they were not doing as well as the ones who were running regular tires.

It all depends upon the track. In some of these coliseum runs you may find yourself running on grass. There is one place in California where the track is all concrete. One nationals race was held on a temporary track built in a horse lot. If you travel around from meet to meet, you never know what kind of track you will find under your wheels.

Some of the factory- or dealer-sponsored riders carry extra wheels and tires they can put on to take care of any local conditions. Riders with rich aunts who dote on them can do the same. The rest of us must do the best we can with what we've got. Of course, if you ride one track all the time, you set up your bike for that.

5. The Power Train

The power to run a bicycle comes from the rider's legs, but something has to change this leg power to rolling-wheel power. The connection between the bottoms of your feet and the rolling wheels is what an automobile mechanic would call "the power train."

If you compare a cycle's operation to that of a car, your legs are the burning gasoline. The pedals are the cylinders that go up and down. The crank is the same as the crankshaft in a car. Your sprockets are the geared transmission. The chain is the drive shaft that transmits the power to the back wheels.

All the breathless pumping in the world is not going to win races for you if too much of your leg power is lost somewhere in the power train.

Pedals

The mechanical power train on a bicycle starts with the pedals. The regular rubber-tread is not quite what you want in BMX. Your foot can slip off it too easily. This is especially true if there is a mud hole or water splash on the track. In such cases the rubber tread on the pedals can get pretty slick. Then your shoes can slip off at some critical point.

The so-called track-racing pedal has teeth along the rims that stop your feet from slipping. It is not a good idea to ride with pedals that have teeth that are too sharp. In some kinds of spills, very sharp teeth can bite into a leg. Teeth do not have to be as sharp as some of them are. For safety's sake you might blunt them down a little with a file. Then there is less danger of tearing your expensive BMX fancy pants.

Unfortunately, pedals stick out where they take a hard bang each time the bike falls. They also are hammered hard by feet pounding out miles per hour. Cheap pedals may break or bend.

Cranks

The crank is the piece of metal that connects the sprocket wheel and the pedal. As your feet go up and down on the pedals, the up-and-down movement is changed to rotary movement by the pedals, crank, and sprocket wheel.

Then the chain riding on the sprocket wheel transmits the power from the pedals to the smaller sprocket wheel on the rear wheel hub. And this is what makes the wheels go around.

The rule that you want strength with lightness holds true here as much as it does in the frame, wheels, and tires.

While bike modifying is not recommended for beginners, the crank is one place where you can improve upon a stock cycle. You can make the crank longer.

In racing you want to be able to move out in a hurry.

The crank is the connecting piece between the sprocket wheel and the pedal.

Since there are no long straightaways where you can hold a high speed for any distance, it is important to move as quickly as you can while you can—especially in getting away from the starting line. You also need to accelerate—pick up speed—as quickly as possible.

The longer the crank, the more pressure you can put on the sprocket wheel to make it turn faster. It is all a matter of leverage.

A lever multiplies force. So it follows that the longer the crank, the more leverage you can put on the sprocket wheel and the faster you can go.

Cranky Cranks

My old friend Tail-End Charlie was aware of this. Charlie's standard 20-incher had stock 5½-inch cranks. Crank measurements are made from the point where the pedal is attached to the point where the crank enters the crank holder.

Now old Charlie was not winning any races. He figured that if he replaced his stock 5½-inch cranks with longer ones he would increase his speed and acceleration. He shifted to 6½-inch cranks, sure that this extra leverage would give him the margin for victory he was after.

The shift to longer cranks did help his acceleration, although he could have gotten the same results by changing his gearing. Charlie was already seeing himself carting home the biggest trophy in the place. And he did quite well until he came to his first sharp turn. He leaned the bike over, rammed out his foot for a fine hot-shoe slide—and the longer crank rammed the pedal into the track. The cycle flipped. Tail-End Charlie—living up to his name—came down on his own tail so hard that he had to sit on a cushion for the next week.

They say one learns from experience. But the smarter person learns from the experience of others. This saves a lot of wear and tear on one's own hide. Well, there is a lesson for us in Tail-End Charlie's sad experience.

Proper Crank Length

This lesson is that crank length must be judged by the necessary ground clearance needed for a leaning turn.

On a straight, flat track you can run long cranks without trouble, but in BMX you must have full crank-to-ground clearance.

This does not mean that you are always stuck with a stock crank. A lot of 20-inch bicycles are deliberately built with low frames. This permits them to be used by younger riders. These low-frame BMX cycles often have 4½-inch cranks as stock equipment. If you try putting a 6½-inch crank on one of these, you are in trouble at the first turn.

You can still run longer cranks by going to cycles with higher frames. To do this you must have legs long enough to reach the ground when you straddle the frame.

The only way you can run long cranks on a low-frame cycle is to cut the frame and raise the crank hanger. This involves welding the parts back in place.

Gearing

Gearing is where you get speed in a cycle. The old-fashioned bicycles had huge front wheels. The pedals were attached directly to these wheels and there was no gearing. Each time the rider's feet made a complete turn of the pedals, the huge wheel made one revolution. The bigger the front wheel, the farther the cycle went for each turn of the pedals.

The invention of the geared sprocket and chain system changed this. It permits you to get several revolutions of the wheels from one revolution of the pedals.

How Gears Work

At this point we have to get a little technical. It takes a bit of mathematics to figure out gear ratios. Mathematics is not a long suit with a lot of us, but figuring gear ratios is not all that difficult. It is extremely important, however. If you are going to race, you need to know about gearing. You'll find this true not only in BMX racing, but in every other kind of wheeled racing you may want to grow into later.

A gear is a round form of a lever. It permits you to multiply force or to increase speed. Incidentally, you cannot have full strength and full speed at the same time. There is just so much power in your legs. By gearing low, you can turn that power into strength for a hard pull, such as up a hill, in mud, or when you are carrying a very heavy load. On the other hand, you can gear high and get the maximum speed.

You can see this illustrated in a car. You are scooting along at top speed in high gear. Then you come to an extremely steep hill. The car starts to labor and slow down. This is because the high gear is ratioed for speed and not for maximum power. You shift down to a lower gear. This gives you greater power but less speed. The extra power that formerly went into giving high speed now is put into overcoming the steep hill.

On a bicycle, the power is transmitted to the back wheel. When you travel in low gear, the back wheel is turning closer to the same number of times that the pedals and the front sprocket wheel are turning. In high gear, the back wheel is turning several times faster than the front sprocket is turning.

The thing to remember is that the lower the gearing, the more power you have. The higher the gearing, the more speed you can achieve.

This is why cars are made with gear shifts, either automatic ones run through oil pressure or the manual kind operated through shift levers. Why don't we use the higher gear and be done with it? Because we must have the more powerful low to get a stopped car moving, and because we may need the more powerful gear to climb steep grades. Once moving, we can shift to a higher gear for more speed.

Bicycle Gearing

Multiple gears for bicycles have not caught on in BMX racing, since there are no hills to climb on a BMX course, and you don't have long straightaways to make the extra speed necessary. Multiple gears could even be a disadvantage because of the time you would lose in shifting gears.

You can achieve the best gearing on your bike by finding the right combination of your front sprocket gear and your back sprocket gear. The front sprocket gear is attached to your pedals. The back sprocket gear is part of the back wheel. The difference in size between these two sprocket gears is called the *gear ratio*. It tells you how many times the back wheel will go around for each revolution of the pedals.

Gearing is created by the difference between the large front sprocket wheel, on the right here, and the smaller sprocket wheel in the rear.

We do not mean diameter when we speak of sprocket sizes. We mean the number of teeth on the sprocket gear wheel. If the front sprocket has forty teeth and the back sprocket has twenty teeth, then one complete revolution of the pedals will make the back wheel revolve twice. This is a two-to-one gear ratio. If the front sprocket has thirty teeth and the back sprocket ten teeth, then we have a three-to-one ratio. This means that the back wheel turns three times for each one revolution of the pedals (front sprocket).

You can see from this that we get more distance for our pedal work when we use a higher gearing. With a three-to-one gear ratio we can go three times as far with the same amount of pedaling as we can with a one-to-one gearing. In a one-to-one gearing the front and back sprockets have the same number of teeth.

Speed Vs. Power

When you run a one-to-one gearing, just about all the power your legs put into the pedals is going through the chain to the back wheel.

We must say "just about all" because we never get all the energy out of a machine that we put into it. Every action eats up some of the energy. The friction of the bearings in the hubs, the rubbing of chain against the sprockets, chains that are too tight or too loose, and even the amount of grease we put on hubs, bearings, and chain—all eat up a bit of the total energy. Thus, not all the pedal power you put into moving the bike reaches the back wheel. Some of it is lost.

We have said that when you run a one-to-one gear ratio you get nearly the same amount of power in the back wheel that you put into the pedals—or as close, anyway, as a mechanical device can achieve. But if you have a two-to-one ratio, the back wheel turns twice as fast for the same amount of pedaling. You do not get twice the power, for you have split the power of one turn of the wheel into two turns. The speed is now faster, but the bike's power is lower. You can go faster, but you cannot climb as steep a hill.

You have not increased power in your legs by going to a higher gear, nor have you lost power. You have only *changed the way you use that power*. If you want more power in the same machine, then pump harder or reduce energy-robbing friction in the moving parts of your bike. Reducing bike weight will also add to the power available.

The Gear for You
Experienced riders agree that there is no one gearing ratio that is exactly right for every track. Also, there is no one gearing ratio that fits every part of a track. So you must strike a balance and work a little harder at your riding.

If you could change gears, you could adjust for various track conditions. For example, you could shift to low for the start when you need power to overcome inertia. (Inertia is just a fancy word that means the vehicle does not want to move. So it takes a bit more effort to get it started.)

Then when you got moving, you could shift to a higher gear and roll along. However, BMX riders tried multigear bikes when the sport first started and then gave them up. They found they lost more time in shifting than they gained by using the extra gears. Then they also found that some of the gear-shifting mechanisms did not stand up well under the punishment of a BMX track.

Also, with most BMX starting lines built on mounds or downhill slopes, gravity helps riders get a fast start, so a low-gear start is not necessary or helpful at all.

Gear Numbers

Riders do not agree on just what is the best combination for all-around gearing. This is not because they are a contrary bunch of jokers. It is just that people are made differently and have different ideas about things. What one person finds is best for him or her may be a disaster for the next rider. You listen to the winning rider, try out that system, and accept it only if it works for you.

Although gearing is a matter of the ratio between the two sprocket wheels, racers do not speak of one-to-one or one-to-three or any other type of ratio gearing. They speak of *gear numbers.*

The use of a gear number shows you instantly the distance ratios of different bikes with different wheel sizes. If the gear number is the same for a twenty-inch bike and a twenty-six-inch bike, then they go the same distance for each crank turn regardless of their differences.

The gear number is found by dividing the number of teeth on the front sprocket by the number of teeth on the rear sprocket wheel. The result of this division is then multiplied by the size of the *back* wheel. The answer is the gear number.

The Right Gear Number

One dealer gave this answer to my question about the right gear numbers for beginners. He said that a good starting point for a ten-year-old of average size might be a gear number of 53.3. A twelve-year-old might ride a gear number of 55.0. Above this age group he recommended that riders try starting out with a gear number of 58.6.

As an example of how gear numbers are figured, let's take the one recommended as a starting point for ten-year-olds. This gear number is 53.3. Suppose we have forty sprocket teeth on our front sprocket wheel and fifteen teeth on the rear one. We divide the 15 into the 40:

$$40 \div 15 = 2.666$$

This figure is the number of times the back wheel will go around for each one revolution of the pedals. Now we multiply this figure by the size of the back wheel in inches. This is always 20 inches for a BMX bike *at this time:*

$$20 \times 2.666 = 53.3$$

The gear number is 53.3, or just what the dealer recommended for the ten-year-old rider.

You don't usually have to do this figuring yourself. Bike shops have gear-number charts that you can consult. All you need to know is the number of teeth on your sprockets and your wheel size. The chart will give you the gear number for various combinations.

Changing the Gearing

It is not difficult to change the gearing on a bicycle. The front sprocket gear is more troublesome than the rear because you must remove the crank, which entails also removing one of the pedals and the chain. When this is done, the old sprocket gear is unbolted. Then you bolt on the new sprocket and reassemble the crank and pedals.

You must remove the back wheel to get at the rear sprocket. Then the sprocket wheel is easily unbolted and a new one put in place. The new combination you use depends upon the results you want. A lower gear ratio gives you more power. A higher gear ratio gives you more speed, but less power.

You are better off in the beginning to run what you have until you are sure that it is the bike and not your lack of experience that is holding you back. Maybe you can borrow a bike with a different gearing. Do you get a better response? Then you can consider changing your own.

If You Must Modify

Bike modification is a hot subject with beginners. Many are not satisfied with their progress—although some lucky ones win from the beginning.

The problem of sticking to what you have is complicated by the flood of gadgets you see advertised in the bike magazines. They run from special frames to friction-reducing hubs.

Some of these special items are very good. As this is written a new sprocket gear has just been introduced. It is made of a special material that includes Teflon, which its promoters say will greatly reduce chain wear. It is also lighter than previous materials. Reports are that it works well, although it has not been out long enough to give us an idea of how it will stand up over the long haul.

First Learn to Ride

There are many ways to modify a bike for racing. For information on this I must refer you to magazines like *Bicycle Motocross Action* and *Minicycle BMX Action*. The latter includes articles on BMX as well as minicycles. The writers are always coming up with new ideas for getting a little more out of a bike than the manufacturer put into it.

This book, however, is for beginners. I do not feel that it is wise for beginners to get into the complicated business of bike modifications. You must learn to race before you really know what you need to change. If you are not winning, changing a gear ratio or buying a new frictionless hub will not necessarily turn a Tail-End Charlie into a Winning Willie. Riding technique is really the most important thing of all.

The best racing machine in the world will not win for you. It can help you win, but it is the rider who wins races. Until you really learn to race, forget about modifications.

After you do learn to race, modifying a bike is a lot of fun. Working out new ideas adds to the interest of racing. And there is a special thrill when one of the ideas works.

Factory Mod Jobs

The above about bike modification is my own opinion. Most racers I talk to agree with me. However, there are some who do not.

"It is the factory race teams on highly modified bikes who are taking home the top nationals trophies," these dissenters say.

I don't think factory team bikes are modified as much as some people think. They do ride the best, and often companies test out new ideas on these team bikes to see if they work, but once they do work, they are put out for sale—after all, that is the purpose of the company.

Also, I must point out that factory-sponsored riders ride in the expert class. They do not compete with beginners or novices. Don't worry about those boys for a while—just learn to ride, and one of these days you may be worrying them.

Therefore, the only modification I recommend for a beginner is to change his gear ratio if he really is dissatisfied with his bike.

6. Tracks, Clubs, and Associations

BMX is just getting started, so there are not as many places to race as there are for motorcycle motocross. However, the sport is growing at the rate of about 15,000 new riders a year. This has brought pressure for more tracks.

The first place to look for the address of a track is in one of the newspapers devoted to the sport. Some of these, like *NBA World*, are devoted only to activities of the National Bicycle Association. This paper is free to members of the association, but some bike shops carry it.

BMX News is a national newspaper which publicizes tracks and special events across the nation. The last issue I saw had 103 tracks listed in twenty-one states. In addition, there are many smaller tracks that are not listed. States where BMX is getting a foothold include Arizona, California, Colorado, Florida, Georgia, Illinois, Indiana, Kansas, Louisiana, Massachusetts, Missouri, Nebraska, Nevada, New Jersey, New York, Ohio, Oklahoma, South Carolina, Tennessee, and Texas.

Some of these meets are business enterprises. The tracks may be additions to regular motorcycle motocross tracks. Some races are put on by promoters. Many are civic enterprises, sponsored by clubs or by local parks and recreation departments. Some are joint activities in which interested parent groups work with clubs or civic groups to provide a place for their children to race.

Sanctioning Organizations

Regardless of who organizes a track, there are two types of operating activity. One is the independent track. This track makes its own rules. The second is the *sanctioned track*—or rather, the *sanctioned race*.

Sanctioning is a word you might as well get used to, for you will hear it as long as you race. It means giving official permission. As it is applied to BMX racing, it means that an organization set up to govern the sport has given a track permission to run a race under the organization's rules.

You will find sanctioning organizations in all motor sports. There is NASCAR, which governs stock-car racing. NHRA is the sanctioning organization for hot rodding. AMA rides herd on a section of motorcycle racing. There are also some competing organizations in these sports.

Purpose of Sanctioning Groups

The general purpose of these associations is to bring standard rules to the sports they govern. You might liken individual tracks to the states of the Union and the sanctioning group or association to the federal government. The states run themselves, but there is the federal constitution to keep them on the track and the federal government to see that they don't get off it.

Now you will always find independent souls who do not want outsiders telling them how to run their tracks. They will make their own rules according to what their riders like.

What's wrong with that? It is their track. As long as the boys and girls who race there are happy, why shouldn't they run the place to suit themselves?

There is nothing wrong with it—*if* their riders are satisfied to ride locally and maybe become the number-one champs of just this one track. On the other hand, if you race under an association's sponsorship on sanctioned tracks, you might—with luck and hard riding—earn enough points to become a national champion someday. The number-one rider is often decided on points gained during the years, since it is hardly possible to bring everybody together for a runoff.

Associations serve other worthwhile purposes as well. They enforce strict safety rules. They demand sportsmanship on the track. They work to expand the number of tracks. They work with manufacturers to improve BMX equipment. Associations are worthwhile. They deserve your support.

The National Bicycle Association

The oldest and largest BMX sanctioning association is NBA—the National Bicycle Association. NBA was formed in 1973 by Ernie Alexander, who was previously deeply into motorcycle sports. Ernie wanted to promote BMX safety to discourage parents from objecting that the sport was too dangerous. He also wanted to provide

The sign above the starting line shows that this is an NBA—
National Bicycle Association—sanctioned race. The Mongoose
sign beside it shows that the race is co-sponsored by the manufacturer of Mongoose BMX products.

a way that riders at various tracks could earn points toward a national championship.

NBA was followed by other sanctioning organizations. IBMX—for International Bicycle Motocross—is
one of them. Its general aims are the same as NBA's.

In addition to the national associations, there are a
number of local sanctioning groups. Often they operate
only within a state or district. These local groups are be-

ing formed all the time as the sport expands. It is difficult because of this to collect the names of them all, but here are some of the best known at the time this was written. The addresses are correct to 1979.

American Bicycle Motocross, 1217 West Hatcher Road, Phoenix, Arizona 85201. Sanctions BMX races in Arizona only.

Bicycle Motocross Association (Arizona), 1822 East Broadway, Tucson, Arizona 85719. Sanctions races in Arizona only.

Bicycle Motocross Association (San Diego), P. O. Box 1970, Chula Vista, California 92010. Sanctions races in the San Diego, California area only.

Florida Bicycle Motocross Association, 70 Melrose Drive, Safety Harbor, Florida 33572. Florida state sanctions only.

National Bicycle League, 1179 S. W. First Way, Deerfield Beach, Florida 33441. Sanctions east of the Mississippi River only.

NPSA-California, 1028 Picadilly Court, Concord, California 94518. Sanctions in California only.

You can expect new organizations to be formed and old ones to close down. These are listed only to show the extent of such groups and the areas they cover. Check with local bike shops that sell BMX equipment. They can give you a line on local associations.

The addresses of the two national organizations are:

National Bicycle Association, P.O. Box 441, Newhall, California 91321

International Bicycle Motocross, P.O. Box 3045, Orange, California 92665

How to Join

The first thing to do is to write the association you might like to join. Find out where they operate and whether they hold any sanctioned races in your area. It does you no good to be a member if you can't ride with others.

This does not mean that the tracks have to be just around the corner from you. In this mobile age, BMX enthusiasts go a long way to ride in their association meets. At an NBA grand national meet in Northridge, California, there were campers with license plates from as far away as Rhode Island.

There is very strong family participation in BMX, with every member helping out. Often they load everybody into a camper, throw the bicycles on top, and make a family vacation out of the trip. If California is the goal, maybe they will stop at Disneyland, and then take in the Grand Canyon as they go back through Arizona.

Membership fees vary. Right now NBA is charging seven dollars a year. For your money, they give you a rule book and a subscription to *NBA World*. This is a very informative newspaper that publishes the standings of members, results of recent races, profiles of teams, schedules of upcoming races, and general information about NBA activities. You also get a membership card and a rating classification that determines the class you will race in at NBA-sanctioned races.

Extra Fees

Your association membership fee in NBA or any of the other national organizations only gives you the right to belong. It does not give you the right to ride on a track unless you pay an entrance fee and meet any additional requirements of the track.

BMX is not yet a big spectator sport, and ticket sales are not enough to pay the expenses and make a profit for the promoters. So tracks have to depend largely upon entrance fees to pay the way. Small tracks may get support from local civic clubs or parks and recreation departments. Some of the larger national meets may get help from various manufacturers. But none of this support is enough—it does help keep the entrance fees lower, but does not do away with them.

Entrance fees may vary from one dollar at a small track sponsored by a parks and recreation group to twelve dollars for a big grand nationals. The bigger meets usually have preentry registration by mail. This can save you as much as 25 percent. This saving is justified because preentries let a promoter know approximately how many riders are coming. They also save time at the track, by cutting down on the number who register just before a race.

Association District Fees

There is another fee you might be required to pay. This is the district fee. The whole country is just too big for any national association headquarters to police by itself. So the national association breaks the country down into districts. Your membership is in the district where you join. If you want to race in another district, then that district will probably ask you for a membership fee to help cover its expenses. The NBA extra-district fee is three dollars.

While each association has its own rules for eligibility, and these are reviewed every year, generally an association will let nonmembers race in its meets just for paying the entrance fee. This may look like a good way for you to save membership costs, but it doesn't work quite as well as that.

Nonmembers will not have an association classification. Tracks do not want an expert stranger "picking cherries" by racing in a lower class, and grabbing an easy trophy against less experienced member riders. Therefore, as a nonmember you would be forced to race in either the expert or open class.

Another point is that as a nonmember you do not accumulate points to establish your national standing.

I must point out, however, that any such standing is valid only in your own association. Since there is no one recognized national association, any "national" rating will be valid only in that association. Thus a rider will be only the NBA or IBMX or XYZ—if there is such an organization—champion.

It might be possible in the years to come to have a final "world series" runoff among the different association champs to find who is really number one in the world. Baseball leagues do this, but the idea has not gotten over into bicycle and motorcycle racing as yet. It would be a terrific promotion deal.

National Tours

One of the most important things associations have brought to BMX are the national tours. These tours are all subject to change or even discontinuation from year to year, but they are doing so well that we can expect them to keep going in some form or another.

As an example of what they are and how they can help you as an individual rider, let's take a look at the 1978 NBA/Schwinn National BMX Tour.

This tour had a combination instruction and race schedule. It was put together by the National Bicycle Association and the people who make the Schwinn cycles. Selected teams ran fourteen races, starting from Los Angeles in late June. They went across country to Washington, D.C., cut south to Florida, and raced at spots in the south and southwest as they worked their way back to L.A. on July 30.

Seminars and Demonstrations

In addition to the races, the touring riders put on a series of seminars and demonstrations at Schwinn dealers along the way.

Races were held (in order of scheduling) in Pueblo, Colorado; Omaha, Nebraska; Chicago; Columbus, Ohio; Pittsburgh, Pennsylvania; Newfoundland, New Jersey; Jacksonville, Florida; Atlanta, Georgia; Chattanooga, Tennessee; Enid, Oklahoma; Ardmore, Oklahoma; Oklahoma City, Oklahoma; Houston, Texas; and Midland, Texas. The races in Newfoundland and Oklahoma City were Schwinn/NBA Nationals races.

Seminars were held in connection with the races in

Omaha, Columbus, Pittsburgh, Newfoundland, Jacksonville, Atlanta, Chattanooga, Oklahoma City, Houston and Midland. In addition seminars were held in these cities where no races were held: Denver, Colorado; Indianapolis, Indiana; Denvill and Millville, New Jersey; and Memphis, Tennessee.

The seminars, which include demonstrations, are a wonderful way to learn the fine points of BMX. The riders are all champions or professionals. They are very good or they would not be on these factory teams. They show you how to slide, start, stop, jump, and—yes—fall on occasion. Often they show you techniques you never thought of.

While even a rank beginner can get much from such seminars, they are of the greatest value to someone who has raced and needs polishing on his or her racing.

These NBA/Schwinn seminars are, of course, not the only ones. Other companies also hold schools for riders, as do associations and sometimes individual clubs that want to expand their memberships. Ask at local bike shops for seminar locations and dates. Also watch the BMX papers for announcements of the bigger ones. If you can't find out about any this way, write to one of the associations and ask where, when, and how you can get in on a seminar.

The Other Side

Associations have been the prime movers in expanding BMX. They have brought us the national races, which would not be possible without big organizations to pull them off. They have worked hard to maintain an excellent safety record for this new sport. They have gone a long way toward standardizing rules, and have worked for better equipment designed especially for BMX.

However, not everybody sees things the same way. We cannot complain about this. After all, it is people disagreeing over who is best that makes races in the first place. So as a result of different viewpoints, there are independent tracks and clubs not affiliated with any association.

The Reasons

When you ask independent clubs why they shun association-sanctioned races, you get various answers.

Some do not agree with association rules and restrictions.

Others say frankly that they can't afford to pay the sanctioning fee. The sanctioning fee is what the association charges the club to run a race under the association's rules. This fee also gives the club the right to advertise that it is an association-sponsored race. NBA, for example, furnishes a sanctioning kit to parks and tracks running under its flag. In the kit are an NBA rule book, score sheets, information about insurance, and other useful material. The NBA might even come out and lend a hand if the sponsoring club is close enough to headquarters.

Another sanctioning organization, the International Bicycle Motocross (IBMX), has much the same program. But in addition, IBMX has a National Travel Fund. This money is used to transport selected winners in various local areas to two nationals races a year. This is a big help.

When these advantages are pointed out to independent tracks, they admit that associations are good for top riders. But independent operators have different purposes in mind.

"The national circuit is a hard grind," one said. "Most of our riders don't have the money or time to follow it. We are putting on races for the local boys and girls who just want a place to have a good time."

Another independent operator said, "Associations have done a lot for BMX. They have done more than any other thing to make it grow the way it has. But they are aimed at the big-time rider. We are devoted to the beginner.

"We had a two-year fight to get our parks and recreation board to let us carve a track here in the park. Then we put a lot of work into building the track ourselves. We did it all. Everybody was a volunteer and still is. We keep our entry fees down to a dollar and all our money goes back into the track. It's our track with our own rules and we want to keep it that way."

This track is strong on beginners, holding classes for them and arranging races where first-time riders compete against each other. This is in addition to the usual beginners' class where the first-timer may be running along with someone who has raced before, but has not progressed from beginner to novice.

First-Timer Races

Such races are held by this club even if there are only two eligible riders. They like to do this because it gives a first-timer a real opportunity to win. Normally, a first-timer who races in a beginners' class is up against riders who have had some experience. His or her chances are not good to win a trophy the first time out. But when first-timers race against each other, one first-timer is bound to win.

Of course, there are really hot first-timers who hit it off from the start. Brent Patterson, who took the Pepsi-Cola West Coast championship in the fifteen-year-old expert class, plus six other championships in his fifteenth year, won the first race he entered.

Association Classes

Association rules are reviewed and revised every year. This is to keep them current and to plug holes in the rules that nobody thought of before. This can cause changes in classifications. While each association has its own rules, in general they classify about the same. Right now the general BMX classes are:

Expert   Riders who have won five or more races.

Novice   Riders who have won at least one race, but less than five.

Beginner   Riders who have never won a trophy.

At some tracks boys and girls race together. Other meets have special girls' divisions. Classes and rules are the same for both.

In addition there is usually an open class or two in which anybody can ride.

Finally, a sidehack race is often held, if there is sufficient interest to bring entrants.

Sidehacks

This race harkens back to the old days of motorcycle racing with sidecars. The sidecar did not want to stay on the ground, and it was the duty of the passenger to keep it balanced. This developed into a specialized form of motorcycle racing, with special low, ground-skimming cycles.

Hack racing is not a part of motorcycle motocross. It is an entirely separate sport. But for some peculiar rea-

A special class is hack racing or sidecars. The passenger's job is to keep the cycle balanced on fast turns. There is no rule against the passenger—called a monkey—getting out and pushing when the pedal pusher finds the going rough.

son or other it has become a part of BMX. In a sidehack race, the riders with their sidecars and passengers use the same course as the regular BMX riders. Sidehack races have become a definite part of the sport, and interest in them is growing.

The sidecar is simply a tube frame attached to the bicycle and connected to a third wheel. It has a platform for the passenger to sit or stand on, and a handhold for him or her to grip.

The Monkey's Antics

In a sidehack race, the passenger is not along just for the ride. He has to work even harder than the dude pumping the pedals. His job is to keep the cycle balanced so the driver can hit the turns, jumps, bumps, and loose dirt at top speed.

Balancing requires him to keep moving all the time. Sometimes he stands. Sometimes he sits or crouches. Or he may almost climb on the back of the cycle with the pedaler. Sometimes you'll see him "hanging it out"— that is, leaning over so far that his behind is almost scraping the ground. In the language of the track—both motorcycle hack racing and BMX—these hard-working passengers are called "monkeys." When you watch them, it is easy to see why.

The Points System

From the standpoint of the individual rider, the most important service provided by an association is the point records that it keeps.

The hack-riding "monkey" has a tough time keeping the fast moving cycles balanced. Here they are really "hanging it out" as they struggle to balance during a fast U-turn.

Each rider belonging to the association is issued a riding number. Every win he makes is recorded in points next to this number. Then, several times a year, the association bulletin or newspaper publishes a list of the standings of its members. That way each rider can see just exactly where he stands nationally with his fellow riders. Since all clubs in the association ride under the same rules, this standing list gives him some idea of how he stacks up as a rider.

The association's top rider, of course, carries the Number One plate. However, there are several other

Number Ones. You can also be Number One in your own club, or in your district, or region, or state. Any of these Number Ones is worth working for. Each is a ladder rung toward the next one.

The Big Bash
The final awards for the association's year may be made at special ceremonies. These are big events, and riders come from all over the nation. The 1977 NBA Awards Night drew over 1,000 people, which shows that a lot of fans came in addition to those being honored.

At this particular event, movies of the top rider of the year were shown, awards were made in all the rider categories, and special awards were made to important behind-the-scenes people. These included Announcer of the Year, Starter of the Year, Photographer of the Year, and Manufacturer of the Year.

The Nationals
You will never gather enough points to get into the receiving line of a grand event like this by riding only in local events. To get enough points, you must get out on the circuit and ride in a lot of national races.

Riding in a national meet is not very different from racing in a local event. The same association rules apply. The track is about the same, as far as obstacles and trials are concerned. The layout will probably be different, because clubs and promoters have to put BMX tracks where they can. The land they use dictates the layout of the track.

A participant's decal on a BMX bike's number plate shows that the rider is officially entered in the Mongoose/NBA Grand National Meet of October 1977. The decal is given after the entrant passes his technical examination. He cannot race without it.

The really big difference is in the competition. If you enter a nationals event, you will be butting horns with the best in the BMX business. A lot more rides on the outcome of these meets than just another trophy to put on the shelf.

Following the nationals circuit is expensive. Most of these top riders could not do it unless they had financial help. This means that they have sponsors, to either foot the bill or to help enough so that they can pull off the rest themselves.

A Beginner and the Nationals

Since the nationals races pull in the best riders from across the country, they would seem to be a poor place for a beginner to compete.

That is certainly true if you are racing the very first race of your life. If you have enough races under your belt to have a general idea of what it is about, entering a nationals event can be a lot of fun, even if you don't have enough experience to win.

Traveling from one nationals to another across the country is pretty expensive, but it is generally possible to enter at least one, for the experience, without traveling too far. The various associations have these events all over the country. Some have more prestige than others, but at all of them you will see riding that is a cut above that at small tracks.

Just sitting on the sidelines and watching some of these nationals contenders is an education in riding.

7. Getting Started

I have already talked about BMX cycles. There is not much more to be said about them. Within the limitations and necessities that I discussed, the most important thing is that you get one you feel comfortable with and can handle easily.

Some riders say they have a little trouble getting used to a bike with a 20-inch wheel after whizzing around the streets on a taller ten-speed cycle. But this is no real problem. After a little practice you'll feel right at home.

The Best Way to Begin

If you are at the stage where you are buying a BMX cycle, then you have already found a place to race and probably mailed in your application for membership in the track club or association.

Now you should watch a few races. I know, you've seen races before, or you would not be wanting to race yourself. But have you *really* watched a race? Before, you were interested in who was going to win. Now that you are going to join in the fun, watch for riding techniques. This time forget about admiring the pretty jackets and swell bikes you see lining up on the mound. Watch how they wait for the starting gate. Where do they position their pedals and their feet for the fastest kind of start? Who got off the starting line first—and why?

You can see who is in the lead, but can you figure out *why* he is ahead? The reason is, of course, that he's better. If you watch him closely, maybe you can spot the little things that make him the top rider in this race.

Watch the way he takes his corners. In every type of wheeled racing, from the Indy 500 to bicycling, you'll find experts who claim that cornering is where races are won and lost. This is not always true, but there is no denying that the rider or driver who can make his turns without losing time has a tremendous advantage over his opponents.

Watch the way he approaches his jumps, how he takes off, the way he shifts his body in flight, and how he touches down. Precious seconds can be lost in not doing things exactly right. In BMX, where a race may be over in forty-five seconds or even less, one second lost in hesitating when you should be plowing ahead can mean the difference between being king or serf at your track.

Watch the jam-ups, as the cycles slow on the corners. You'll often see some smart rider come out of these traffic jams better than the others. Frequently a Tail-End Charlie will flank the others on an outside turn—or take advantage of a hole the others missed and slip through to take the lead. He can do this because he has a quick eye and because—most important of all—*he knows what to look for.*

That is what you are out there watching to learn. Never mind getting caught up in the excitement of the race. Watch for the *how* and the *why* of the best riders.

Learn from the Losers Too

You learn hot riding techniques by watching the winner, but you can learn some good lessons from the losers as well. After you learn what to watch for, you can spot errors. They hit you right in the face.

You'll find yourself saying, "He let himself get boxed in on that turn," or "He pulled it too high on that jump." In this way you are storing up racing experience even before you take to the track yourself.

And once you do start racing, don't stop watching. At races you will see riders who never watch the others. When not racing or when waiting their turn in the staging area, they tinker with their bikes, rap with others, or go hunt the hot-dog stand. But you'll see others who sit with their eyes glued to the track. These are the ones who believe in learning by the experience of others. These are serious ones who will cause you the most trouble on the track.

The Last Two Seconds

In a recent BMX race I watched a determined rider get ahead at the start. He kept his small lead through the turns, jumps, and obstacles. Then, as he turned into the final straightaway, heading for what he and I thought was a sure trophy, the number two man put on a dazzling burst of speed. He inched up and sped ahead in the final two seconds of the race. The boy who had led the pack through the entire race took the flag second, wondering what had happened.

The answer was simple enough. In pure racing technique the winner did not outrace his opponent. They were pretty even there, although the loser had done a bit better in getting off the starting line first.

The winner took the trophy on stamina. He just flat outlasted the other. He had enough reserve strength to put on a final sprint of speed when the leading rider was either just holding his own or beginning to falter.

Shape up or Lose out

BMX is a sport, and in any competitive sport you cannot hope to win unless you get in shape for it. This means a strong and continuous physical conditioning program.

Strength alone is not the deciding factor. You have to know how to race. But you must remember that every bit of power that goes into spinning your bike's wheels comes from your own legs. The hot-rod racers and the motorcycle jockeys have horsepower to help them around the track. You have only your leg power. Lungs and legs are what count when you pass the three-quarter mark and need that extra burst of speed to move into the lead.

To see how important an athletic body can be, consider these qualifications of thirteen-year-old Alex Bogusky, who was NPSA-Florida state BMX champion in 1977. He held the Presidential Physical Fitness

Award—gold, silver, and bronze medals in skiing—and was a first-string soccer player until BMX got to taking up too much of his time. On top of that, he was an honor student.

Different Styles

As I talk to different winners, I see that there is no set style for conditioning yourself physically for BMX. Many have their own styles. Some don't even bother. They were born junior Tarzans, I suppose. The majority, however, take keeping in shape very seriously. If they did not at first, it took only a couple of exhausted finishes to convince them to do so.

One champ runs several miles a day. Another agrees that this is a powerful builder of legs and wind, but argues that it should be done on a cycle. "I spend every minute I can on my bike," he says. "I get the extra training in bike handling."

Another invested $150 in a cycle exerciser. These have been around for a long time, used for general exercise in building up legs, heart, and lungs. An exerciser is just a bike with no back wheel and a weighted front wheel on a stand. You can pump all day and go nowhere. The better kind has a speedometer and odometer so you can tell how fast and how far you would have gone—if you had been going. They work very nicely for practice indoors when you can't get out in the open.

Not all of us can afford such luxury. If you need one, perhaps you can build a stand to keep your back wheel

Reserve strength is what lets one rider pull ahead of the others at the finish of a race. This is the result of a lot of riding and a good calisthenics program.

off the ground and use your regular bike. This is better anyway, for you practice with the machine you'll be racing. The stand should be strong, however. You don't want it collapsing on you.

Back Yard Practice

Just plain, straight street riding or pedaling an exerciser helps build strength and stamina. It does not give you practice in specialized racing techniques. This you can get only on the BMX track. Unless you have the space —and few do—to set up a track in your backyard, you are restricted to what little practice you can get during the practice runs before the weekend races.

Even if there is a track close enough for you to pedal over in the evenings, you won't be able to get in. Unsupervised riding can lead to accidents. If riders start getting hurt, insurance rates balloon and the track is shut down.

If you can find an empty lot or field where you can practice jumps and turns, you are very fortunate. But never use vacant lots or land for practice without asking permission of the owner. Otherwise they have the right to lodge trespass charges against you.

Some riders, faced with the problem of a place to practice, have rigged up individual hazards in their backyards. There is never enough space, but it is possible to put in one jump or one turn. This can give you a lot of practice that can be helpful on a real track.

I know one rider who rigged a banked turn in one corner of his backyard. Then, by leaving the gate open and starting at the street, he could charge alongside the house, flash through the gate and hit his backyard turn at full racing speed. He credited it with really putting a fine tune on his cornering.

Of course, he had an argument with his mother, who wanted the space for a flower bed, but he was quite a talented debater.

No Street Racing

The one place you do *not* practice racing techniques is in the street. For one thing, your racing bike, with its fenders, reflectors, and other required equipment removed, is not street legal. Hot shoeing around corners, jumping off curbs, and hitting top speed on the road can get you a ticket for reckless driving. On the street a bicycle rider is no different from an automobile driver.

Recently in California a skateboard park added a place where BMX riders can practice for a fee. It is hoped that more of these will open up as the sport grows.

The Tech Inspections

Before you can race, your bike must be inspected. In BMX this is really more of a safety inspection than a technical inspection. In hot-rod and motorcycle technical inspections, examiners look for illegal modifications and check to see that the car or cycle technically fits the classification for which it is entered. A bicycle is so small and open that there is not much you can hide. As long as it has a 20-inch wheel and looks right, you can generally get by technically.

The safety check part is something else. While the thoroughness of the inspection depends upon the track and the examiner, they do often bear down on this. BMX has a reputation for being a safe sport, as wheeled sports go. The officials are eager to keep it that way.

If the race is association sanctioned, then the tech inspection will follow association rules. Even so, how thorough it is will depend upon the experience of the examiner.

Inspection Checklist

The following checklist for a tech inspection was given to entrants in an NBA/Mongoose (BMX Products, Inc.) nationals:

1. Check for cracks in bars, goosenecks, frames, and cranks.
2. Check wheels for cracks and loose or broken sprockets.
3. Check wheel axles. The ends of the bolts must not stick out more than ¼ inch beyond the retaining bolts.
4. Bikes must have brakes that will lock the wheel.
5. Safety pads must be in place over the crossbar and the gooseneck.
6. The regulation "pie plate" must be in place. Your association number must show clearly. (This means that you will have to put your decals somewhere else.)

Most track rules demand that crossbars and goosenecks be covered with padding. Rules such as these ensure track safety.

7. Riders will be checked for elbow pads or long sleeves, safety helmets, and shoes. (Yes, there are those who would race barefooted if they could.)

Other Things to Check

This checklist is only an outline. Actually the inspectors look for other things as well. Here are some things that are sure to get eyeballed at almost any track:

1. Tires must be in good condition. No baldies or cracked casings. Knobby tires are preferred, but may not always be required.
2. Grips must be tight on the ends of the handlebars. No metal is permitted to show beyond the ends of the grips.
3. Pedals must be in good condition. Check for cracks and wear. Most tracks do not require metal pedals, but if you run rubber ones, they must not be worn so badly that your foot cannot get a good grip.
4. The seat must be tight.
5. The frame, in addition to being checked for cracks, may be inspected for strength. Yes, it takes more strength to push a heavier bike around the track, and light weight is now the big catchword in BMX racing. But there is such a thing as being too light. For example, you might save a half pound of weight by sawing off the crossbar between the handlebars, but you can rest assured that if you do, the tech inspector will saw your name right off the list of entrants. Weight saving is fine, but not at the expense of sensible safety.

All of these rules make sense. Every one was framed

to make the race safer for you and for the other riders. If you break down on the track, it could cause one or several others to upset along with you.

Avoid Disqualification

There's no question about it. It is a blow to come out all hepped up to win a race and have a tech inspector say, "No way!"

This disappointment can be easily avoided by making your own safety check before coming to the track. I will discuss this more fully in the chapter on bike care.

Right now it is sufficient just to say that your safety check has to be made correctly. For example, you know that axle bolts may not stick out more than a quarter of an inch beyond the bolts. This is to prevent a leg getting torn by the bolt if the rider hits it in a spill.

Yet, at a tech inspection I heard a rider arguing loudly against his disqualification. "I cut the bolt off!" he yelled. "You can see it! There's not over a quarter of an inch sticking out!"

And he had taken a hacksaw and gnawed the bolt off to the proper length. But that is all he did. The edges of the cut bolt were burred and knife sharp. If he had hit his leg against the bolt in a spill, it would have ripped his flesh worse than the original bolt.

A poor correction is no correction at all.

Practice Runs

Tracks open early to permit practice. Since so many of you do not have a suitable place to practice, you must take advantage of every minute you can stay on the track before the race begins. These practice sessions are as important as the race itself, and can make the difference between winning and losing.

Here is where you find out how fast you can take the turn without spilling, how to take advantage of holes in order to charge from the back to get into the lead, how to jump to the best advantage, and how much you must brake before going into the rough whoop-de-dos.

No matter what kind of a practice run you may have set up at home, track practice will help you more than any other. For one thing, you are practicing on the exact course you will be racing on. Secondly, you are not the only rider out there. You are getting experience in actual racing.

Learning the Track

Since these practice runs are races in themselves, a beginner is usually out to win. This may be a mistake.

That may seem like a strange statement to make. After all, the object of racing *is* to win. But the practice run is not a real race. It is *practice*. Winning here brings you no trophy and no points. A win may help your ego, but the important thing in practice is to *learn*. If you concentrate too hard on winning, you may overlook the things practice is for.

For one thing, you want to know the condition of the track. If you have never been on this course before, you want to know how to ride it. If you have raced the track before, then you want to know if and how it has changed since the last time. Rains or baking sun may have changed parts of it. That corner that was so loose the last time may be hard and more difficult to take at a fast speed this time. If you rely on what happened the last time you ran it, you might find yourself in a pileup because you tried to take it just a bit too fast.

The same thing holds true of the rest of the track. In a practice run you can push your luck to see just how far you can go. If you do make it, then you know what you can do. If you take a flop, then you have learned that you'll have to take it easier on that particular jump when the real race begins.

Walking the Track

There is a gimmick you can pick up from motorcycle motocross riders. A lot of them report that they get out and walk around the track before they make their first practice run.

"In this way I can see things that I might miss riding around the track," one said. "What I am looking for is the best line around the corners. I also look for the smoothest part of the track. Let the others hug the inside and get jammed up. I want to know how the berm [that is, the ridge of dirt on the outside of a turn] is, so I can swing out wide at a faster speed if I have to.

"I plan my whole run on that walk," he went on. "Then when I make my first practice run, I don't pay one bit of attention to the rest of the riders. I could care less if they pass me by. I am studying the track, following the line I've chosen and trying to figure out if I was right about it.

Practice is where you learn the track. You should get as many practice runs as possible.

"Sometimes I'm not and I make changes. Then, after I understand the track, I start paying attention to the other riders."

A Line on Your Opponents

When this rider spoke of paying attention to the other riders he hit on an important point overlooked by many beginners. If you know something about the racing styles of the other riders, you will have a decided advantage.

What you want to do here is find out which of the other riders you think will give you the most trouble. Then you watch him, seeking his merits and faults. Is he cautious on the jumps? If so, maybe you can risk a little more speed in making your own. Does he insist on hogging the inside on all turns? Or is he one of those who likes to swing wide on the berm, taking the long way around in the hope he can make up in speed what he loses in footage?

Take Advantage of His Weaknesses

Once you know your toughest opponent's weaknesses, you can use this knowledge to figure out how to take advantage of them. You can do this not only by taking advantage of his poor techniques to get ahead at certain points, but also by pacing your own shortcomings.

For example, suppose you have all sorts of trouble getting a good ride through the rough whoop-de-dos. You have been upsetting because you try to hit the roughs too fast. You know you have to slow down. The question is, how much can you afford to slow without losing the race?

If you know your opponents' weaknesses on other parts of the track, then you can figure out how much you can slow on the roughs and expect to make the time back on the hazards where you are better. Maybe that is in the jumps, or the turns.

Help from the Sidelines

Another rider admitted the value of knowing your opposition, but said he didn't have time to do it on the track.

"I don't get enough practice runs," he said. "I've got all I can do to figure my line on the track. But I have a big brother who races in the seventeen-and-up class. When I make my practice runs he makes a point of being there and watching.

"When I come in after a run he is right there to tell me: 'That dude riding number 15 is the one you've got to beat. I know he didn't come in first on this practice run, but he wasn't trying. He was feeling out the track. He's good.'

"And he also tells me what I did wrong. That is very important. When you are out there pumping for all you're worth, you don't always spot your own mistakes. You really need a spotter in the beginning."

Open Track

At the track, a lot of people want to ride. So there has to be some control. You will not be allowed to roll your bike out on the track and take off whenever you please.

Most tracks—for control and safety purposes—will not let you on the track until the announcer calls for practice. Then it is just like a race. The starter calls each class of riders for practice. You wait in the staging area and come up on line when you are called.

This is good, in that you are not just rolling around the track. You are getting practice and experience under actual racing conditions. It is bad in that you probably will not get more than a couple of practice runs if there is a large field of riders that day. You need more than this. You can never get enough practice.

One answer to the practice problem is to enter every race you can. If they will let you, enter twice. Enter once in your age and experience classification and again in the open class if this is possible. Never mind that you are outclassed in the open. You are in it for practice and experience. If you can get enough of both and have a true fighting spirit, the wins will come as a matter of course.

8. Riding Techniques

Do you really know how to ride your bike? You may think that you do. In fact, you may do very well in ordinary riding. But racing is something else again. Faults that ordinarily mean little can cut seconds off your time in a race. And when you have just slightly over half a minute to get all the way around the track, every second is precious.

Body Position in Riding
In other kinds of bicycle riding—touring, track racing, and the like—teachers put great emphasis on body position. They point out that this is important because the way you sit can lessen fatigue. Your body position can also make it harder or easier to pedal. In fast track or road racing, poor body position can act as a brake to reduce your speed.

This is due to air resistance. If you sit upright, the wind against your body slows you down. You have to pedal harder to overcome the resistance. This is why you see road and track racers crouching low over their handlebars. In this way they present less of their body to air resistance.

The problem of the correct body position in BMX is

somewhat different. In this kind of racing, speed is not always the most important thing. The nature of the track is such that you can never go full speed for any length of time, as you can on an oval or flat track. In motocross as soon as you get a straightaway it suddenly turns into a sharp corner, a jump, a mudhole, a sandy strip, or a whoop-de-do.

You can't take all of these at full speed. There is a lot of slowing down in motocross. This makes acceleration very important. The joker who can get from slow to fast in the quickest time is going to be the hot shoe you have to beat.

A good rider who accelerated sluggishly could overcome that disadvantage on a long straight track. But in motocross there are too many times when you have to accelerate. You can't make up for all the time losses. You must be able to go from slow to fast *fast*.

This means that you won't be sitting on the seat of your bike very much. You'll be standing on the pedal so you can throw the full force of your body into powering your bike. Yes, in this way you are presenting more body surface to the air you are hitting, but it can't be helped.

Jerky Pumping

If you watch at the end of the first straightaway, you can see very clearly the right and the wrong way to pump a bicycle.

In the case of the better riders, the front wheel is moving straight down the track. In the less skilled

In BMX racing you don't spend a lot of time sitting on the seat. You are standing on the pedals, pumping for all you are worth. This is a sixteen-and-over racing class.

riders, the front wheel is weaving in a jerky side-to-side movement.

Each time the front wheel weaves, the rider is adding a fraction of an inch more to the track. A straight line is still the shortest distance between two points. That is one law nobody has been able to break.

The jerkiness you see is caused by the rider's full weight shifting back and forth between the pedals. Watch a jerky rider's body and you can see it shift and weave under the force of his downward pressure. He is putting too much into it.

What you have to work for here is more smoothness in your pedaling.

If you throw all your weight on a pedal and then frantically shift your full weight to the opposite pedal when the first gets to the bottom, you cannot help but get a jerky ride. The back-and-forth swing of your body, in addition to the shifting of pressure on the pedals, forces the bike into a jerky movement.

Knee Positions

The faster you go, the more this jerkiness smooths out. Unfortunately, it's worst during acceleration, when it hurts you the most.

One way to help cut down jerkiness is to watch the position of your knees and legs. The knees should be pointed straight down the track and held in close to the bike frame. If they stick out, then the power of your body does not flow in a straight line down to the pedals. You are not getting all the power your legs can put out. If you walk with your toes turned out, you may be riding the same way. This turnout has a tendency to pull your knees off the straight line they should maintain. Put your feet solidly and squarely on the pedals so your knees point straight.

Then try not to swing your body back and forth as

you transfer from one pedal to the other. As you certainly know, you can turn a two-wheeled vehicle by leaning in the direction you wish to go. If you lean your body in shifting your weight from one pedal to the other, you are nudging the bike to go first in one direction and then in the other. When this happens, it is understandable that the bike becomes confused as to just what line you want it to take. This is when you start wobbling that front wheel.

Let Your Ankles Do the Work

You might think that this is a small thing. Perhaps the extra bit of power you lose by weaving is more than made up by the acceleration. However, if you ride properly, you can get that extra power without throwing it away in weaving losses.

You see, the pedals of a moving bicycle travel in a circle. If you press one pedal to the bottom and then shift your weight to the opposite pedal and press it down, you are using each pedal for power only through a part of the full circle that it must turn.

That's okay, you say. This is all I need, because my other foot takes over the job as the first one finishes. I am applying power through the full circle turn of the sprockets.

This is true—but you can apply power through more than just a half turn with each foot. You do this by proper use of your ankles, as road and track bicycle racers do. This means that there is a time when you are using both feet, instead of one always working alone while the other waits its turn.

This racing technique is called "ankling." Although it is standard technique in other types of racing, for some odd reason many BMX beginners do not seem to have heard of it. It is something you should know, for it not only increases power to the pedals but helps smooth out the jerkiness caused by body shift from pedal to pedal.

The Ankling Technique

When you push down, first on one foot and then on the other, your leg is moving up and down.

Now, since the pedal, and the sprocket wheel attached to it, are traveling in a circle, you want to make your feet do the same. This stops the jerkiness and keeps an even tension on the chain so that the rear wheel turns smoothly.

Here are the steps in the ankling process:

1. Beginning at the top of the circle when the pedal is straight up, your foot is square on the pedal.

   Learn to operate from the ball of your foot, letting the pressure come from this part of the foot.

2. As you press—not jerk or jam—your foot down to move the pedal, raise your heel while maintaining pressure from the ball of your foot.

3. As the sprocket wheel and pedal rotate, keep raising your heel. At the bottom position your foot is in much the same position as when you are trying to stand on tiptoe.

This position is as far down on the pedals as you could get with your feet flat and your legs straight up and down.

4. At this point, with your foot bent at the ankle as much as possible, rotate the pedal and press *backward* and *upward* with your foot. You're giving an extra push with this leg.

5. When you have shoved backward as far as you can, let up on the pressure with this foot.

6. Bring your heel down and raise your toes—still on the rotating pedal—as high as you can.

7. Then, as the other foot is pressing down in the manner described above, press your cocked foot *up* as soon as the pedal gets close enough to the top for you to do so.

When the pedal gets to the top again, start rotating your ankle to make the cycle all over again.

What Ankling Does

What you are doing here is giving an extra push at the end of the leg stroke and starting the upward push earlier.

Since the power to move the cycle comes from your pushing legs, the extra amount of push adds more power. Instead of one leg working at a time, there is a short period at the top and bottom of each stroke when both legs are providing power.

This may not be much, but it all helps. Some racers claim that ankling can increase their drive per leg to over 200 degrees. A full circle is 360 degrees. A half circle is 180 degrees. Thus they claim to add 20 degrees in which full power is obtained.

Even if you don't get this much, ankling is a valuable racing technique which you should learn. It makes for a smoother flow of power by eliminating a lot of jerky pumping. A lot of races are decided by a nose, and just this little bit more power may make your nose the one that gets the checkered flag first.

It Takes Some Getting Used to

Ankling is not difficult, but it does take some practice to get the technique down smoothly. The best way to start is to begin very slowly. Pedal as slowly as you can and still keep upright. Then after you get the idea and can swing your foot at the ankles in the correct way, begin speeding up a *little*. An exercise bike, which is stationary mounted, is an excellent means of practicing ankling. It permits you to start slowly and get the feel of ankling.

Take it easy, increasing speed as you get used to the different swing of your feet. The important thing is to pedal smoothly and with rhythm. So learn to ankle right and then gradually step up your speed. The ankling technique, which is awkward at first, will come to you quicker than you think. You will immediately see an improvement in your riding.

It's Tough on the Ankles

One reason you don't see more ankling among beginning BMX riders is that the technique is tough on the lower leg and foot muscles at first. Many who try it give up too quickly, saying, "This is not for me. It makes things worse."

It is just that you are bringing muscles into play that you don't ordinarily use. Naturally they are awkward and get sore at first. Keep at it. As in any other thing you try for the first time, the aches will go away as your muscles get accustomed to the different movements. Then you will find that ankling is a real friend on the track.

Toe Clips

Toe clips are metal cages that attach to your rattrap (all-metal) pedals. Whether or not you can race with toe clips depends upon track rules. Inquiries I made at various tracks mostly brought the answer, "You can run them if they are a kind your foot can slip out of easily if you fall. We don't want anybody getting hurt."

Toe clips are not as important in BMX as they are in road racing. But there are two reasons you might want to use them. One is that they force you to keep your feet straight on the pedals. The cage imprisons your toe, and your foot can't slip forward or turn out on the pedal. You keep riding on the ball of your foot as you should.

More importantly, a toe clip lets a rider apply foot power through the entire circle of the pedals. In that part of the power circle when you can no longer press down even with ankling, you can continue to apply pressure by an upward pull of your foot against the toe clip. In this way you apply pressure through the entire

Toe clips are cages made of metal and strap that fit around the toe of a rider's shoe. They permit him to pull up as well as push down on the pedal, increasing the time that power can be applied.

360 degrees of the pedal movement. Proper ankling and toe clips let a rider double the amount of power applied to the pedals as compared to one who just pumps down,

shifting his weight from pedal to pedal. At the same time, you get a smoother, more even transfer of power from legs to pedals.

Objections to Toe Clips
A lot of riders don't like to use toe clips. They can't slip their feet out of them fast enough when they fall.

According to one rider, "They're okay for track racers. They don't fall as much as motocross racers. I don't want anything holding me to the cycle when I go down."

Another said, "I don't think you need them in motocross. Speed is not the important thing. Gear your bike for the best acceleration. That's where races are won or lost."

Still another, with the best argument of all, said, "I don't need 'em. I'm winning now. I don't want to add something else that I have to get used to."

On the other hand, you will find those who like them and feel that toe clips are a big help.

Personally, I feel that they are for experienced riders. When you have learned to ride well—and most importantly, can fall without getting your feet caught in the clips—you might experiment with toe clips.

Psyching
You hear a lot of talk on the tracks about *psyching*. The word psyching comes from "psychology" and it means trying to convince your opponents that they can't possibly win against you. Or at least making them worry

about it. This supposedly gives the "psycher" a mental advantage.

One way this is done is to show more confidence than you feel. One top rider reports that he does deep knee bends just before going to the starting line. Another says he deliberately yawns, as if the competition bores him.

Still another said, "I know practice runs are to let you get the feel of the track and a win means nothing in the way of points. But I go wheels out to win anyway. I bust my heart out to come in first. I think it psychs the others. I want them to get the idea that they don't have a chance against me in the real race."

What Good Is Psyching?

Does psyching do any good? It is hard to say. When you have a really big race going, riders who really want to win badly can get pretty nervous. It does not take much to shake some of them up. This can make them take chances or slip into errors that can hurt their chances of winning.

One coach told me that he was in favor of psyching. "I don't think my boy scares a soul with his psyching tactics. But he thinks that it does and that helps *him*. Anything a rider can do to raise his own confidence is good in my book. So if my boy is psyching himself instead of the other fellow, that's great."

On the other hand, psyching can work the other way too. You can scare the other rider so badly that he puts out more. This could leave you eating his dust when the checkered flag is waved at the end of the race.

Anyway, trying to psych the other riders is worth a try—if you don't overdo it. No one likes a braggart and a showoff.

The Start

Earlier I talked about the mechanical part of starting. I discussed starting gates, rubber-band starts, and flag starts. I also mentioned something about watching the flagman and the staging areas. At this point I will talk about the technique of a good start.

A good start is important, but it is not the total race. Many riders have made poor starts and overcome the disadvantage farther down the track. However, a good start gives you an advantage that the others have to overcome.

Spacing

The first point in a good start is to be sure there is enough space between you and the cyclists on either side of you. Unfortunately, a lot of spacing trouble in a start is caused by things you have no control over. You need space to maneuver in. The width of the track and the number of riders entered in your moto will determine the space you get.

There should be at least a foot between handlebars, but I've seen them packed closer. Packing is often seen at big races where there are a large number of riders. A little squeezing is necessary to get everybody in.

Picking Your Place in Line

The inside of the track is always the shortest distance around. Horse-race jockeys and other oval-track racers —auto, motorcycle, bicycle and even runners—love the inside position. Motocross, with its right and left turns, is a little different. The inside changes from turn to turn. If you want to keep the inside on every turn, you will have to switch sides of the track.

During your practice runs you have decided upon a certain line as the best way around the first turn. You want a position in the starting line that will let you get into this line as quickly as possible.

In some races you are assigned your starting position. But most of the time it is first come, first served. When your group is called, move quickly to get the place you want.

In a beginners' race, where there may be a lot of weaving, the end position is often the best. Then you have to worry about only one rider bumping you at the start.

The Mechanics of Starting

No one can tell you exactly how to start. This is something each rider must figure out for himself. It depends a lot on one's personal riding style.

Track rules don't say much about how you must start. They sometimes say you must have one foot on the pedals. This would surely be the case anyway. Just where you locate the pedal for a pushoff depends upon what you find is best for you.

Some want the pedal all the way to the top so they get a longer push for that first kickoff.

I've talked to others who feel they can get better leverage if the pedal is three-quarters of the way down. The argument here is that they can get more weight on their leg if their knee is not drawn up so high. This lets them put more strength into the initial push, starting the wheel spinning faster.

Just how much difference this makes is a matter of personal opinion. If you experiment around, you'll find what is best for you. It is important to remember that what another finds best may not be the best for you.

Whatever you do should be comfortable and should become automatic. At the beginning of a race your mind should concentrate on the starter. If you have to think about your mount, your attention is divided. You have not had enough practice to make the mechanics of starting as automatic as it should be.

The Push-off

You start with one foot on the pedal and one on the ground. But *which* one *where*? You know that people are right-handed or left-handed. But is there such a thing as left- or right-legged?

Yes, most people do better with one leg than the other. It may be that you are more comfortable starting with a particular leg. This is the foot to use, for you want your every action to flow easily without effort.

While the foot you place on the starting pedal and the position of the pedal itself are important, the foot you have on the ground is equally important. This is the one that gives you a shove to help you get started. You want to make it work for you. Therefore, do not just bear down on the pedal with one foot and shove off with the other. Study these movements, trying to find the places to put your feet to give you the best racing support.

The Lineup

You must line up on the starting mound with your wheel pointed straight down the track. In the excitement of starting, a lot of beginners forget this. They weave at the start, trying too hard in their eagerness to get moving fast. They shift weight from pedal to pedal. This can throw them to one side, bumping another rider. Such bumping, if it does not cause upsets, can still slow both riders.

Your legs do the pumping, but you actually race with your entire body. That big behind of yours, shoved back, can put more weight on the rear wheel to make it dig deeper. You can lean your trunk forward and shove down on the handlebars to prevent the front wheel from coming up in a wheelie.

Wheelies look cute, but this is something you do not want on the starting line. Even though the back wheel is the only one that is powered, the front wheel also digs in and helps pull you along. You want that wheel on the ground working for you. Also, you cannot steer with the front wheel in the air.

Your body can help you along in other ways. Motorcycle riders call this "body English." It has to do with the way you shift your body for balance and control. Body English is especially important in jumping.

Recovery from a Poor Start

A poor start can happen to the best of riders at times. It can be caused by carelessness. It may be the fault of a poor rider who bumps you. Or it can be just plain bad luck.

But whatever causes it, a bad start does not have to be a total disaster. Riders have gotten up from a full sprawl and gone on to win races. The secret is fast recovery. I know one rider who practices falls. He is now an expert at getting back in the race in record time.

9. Running the Race

In a horse race, a bicycle race, or even a foot race, contestants don't always like to get out in front at the start. They say you are burning up energy that you should be conserving to pull ahead in the stretch.

Motocross, however, is not the same as these other races. The difference lies in the short straightaway between the starting line and that first sharp turn. As the front-runners slow down to make the turn, there is a pileup of riders behind them. The riders in front set the pace and cut off those in back. So if you are in front or close to it, you're less likely to get hemmed in.

Cornering
Many riders will tell you that motocross races are won or lost in the turns. This is not exactly true. You can lose a race anywhere along the track, and you have to fight every inch of the track to win. But there is no denying the extreme importance of cornering. When bikes bunch up and slow down on these turns, the sharp-eyed rider who can spot an opening and take the turns faster is going to come out with an advantage that the rest will find hard to overcome.

The number of riders in a moto determines how much

On narrow turns there is often a traffic jam that boxes in the riders in the back. This is why a fast start is important, so this will not happen to you on the first turn.

of a jam there will be on this first turn. Usually the jam is worse here than on the other turns because the riders haven't begun to string out yet. Usually they are still running pretty close together.

If this is a beginners' race, someone may fall. One of the front-runners, not yet able to gauge how fast to make a turn, may find his bike slipping out from under him. If he falls, then there is frantic maneuvering by those coming behind to keep from piling on top of him.

This is why following another rider is a poor way to race. You have no space in which to maneuver. In fast bicycle track racing it is often good strategy to follow another rider. He breaks the air for you. Since you get less air resistance, following is less tiring for you. Then, when the rider you are following tires at the end, you can sprint on ahead.

But this is not that kind of a race. Make a rule here and now: Never follow!

The Best Line
The inside of a track is the shortest distance around a turn. It is also the sharpest curve. At the same speed you are more likely to trip up on the inside than on the outside of a track.

When you look at a curved track, the outside line does not appear to be so much longer than the inside that you need to be concerned about it. However, let's take a look at the drawing below. Line A–B shows the inside track of a sharp turn. Line C–D shows the outside track of the same turn. Line E–F shows a straighter line through the turn. It swings from the outside at E to the inside of the curve and then back outside to F.

Now if we use a flexible, curved ruler and measure these three curved lines and redraw them as straight lines, we get the three straight lines shown at the bottom of the figure.

You can see immediately that line A–B—the inside track—is much shorter than the outside line C–D. Line E–F, cutting across the track, is shorter than the outside line, but a little longer than the inside line.

The actual difference in length between these lines

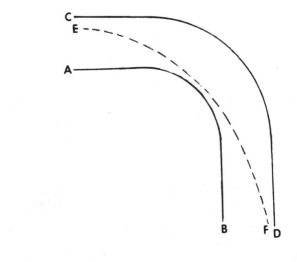

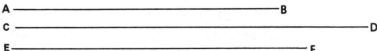

While the inside line of a turn is the shortest distance around, as a comparison between these three lines shows, you can do better sometimes by following a swing from outside to inside and back to outside (line E–F), for it produces a less sharp turn. This permits you to run the curve at a faster speed. You can only do this if track conditions are right.

will vary according to the width of the track; the wider the track, the greater the difference will be.

While many riders like the inside track because it is shorter, it is not always the best line to take. Sometimes it is better to take line E–F because it is straighter and you can pedal faster than you can making a sharper turn like A–B. You can take a line like E–F only if the track is open; that is, with plenty of room. You don't want to get boxed in behind somebody; doing so will slow you down.

Traffic on the track will often dictate which line is best to use. So many riders try for the inside track that there is often a traffic jam here. In that case, you can sometimes take the outside line and get around faster than everyone else except the front runners.

This is one of the things that makes racing exciting. You can't figure out everything in advance. You have to do some split-second thinking in these tight spots, and how well you do it often means the difference between failure and a trophy.

The Surge

Consider the situation shown on page 156. On a narrow track these six riders have just come down a steep hill leading from the starting line. Now they are beginning to go into the first turn. The front riders are slowing up to what they think is a safe speed to get around the corner without spilling. The three back riders are cut off, especially the two on the inside (right).

But notice number 915. He sees an opening between cycles 479 and 1716. You can tell his supreme effort by the position of his body. Between his seat and the seat of the cycle there is air. Look at his arms and fists. There is no laxness there. You can see that he is putting out a greater effort than the others. He is throwing everything he has into the pot, to come up through that hole and take the lead.

Number 915 sees a hole and is preparing to surge through it. The position of his body shows his extra strength.

Although the term is not used in motocross, in track bicycle racing this is called *surging,* a term that comes from England. It means suddenly throwing all you have into a do-or-die attempt.

Hot Shoes and Berms

Anytime you try to make a surge in a turn, there is a strong chance that you are begging for an upset. A smart rider here is trying to slow down to what he thinks is a safe speed. What little you gain by recklessness is lost if you slip and have to make a fresh start while the others race ahead of you.

There are ways that a knowledgeable rider can get around a corner a bit faster than the play-it-safe boys. One of the ways is to learn to judge turns so that you know exactly how fast you can go into one without upsetting. Then you approach the turn at top speed, brake down to the fastest safe speed, and follow the line you selected in your practice runs.

Then, in making the actual turn, you may want to do a little hot shoeing. This is a standard cornering technique. As you make your turn, take your inside foot off the pedal and extend it to brace the cycle if you start to fall. This permits you to take a turn at a faster speed than you could otherwise.

Remember this, however. In motorcycle racing an engine is pulling the cycle and rider along. Sticking out a foot does not lessen the rider's power in any way. But when you are racing with pedal power, anytime you take your foot off the pedal you are coasting. So the rule here is to keep your foot on the pedals, pumping away for all you are worth, for as long as you can.

This does not mean that you should not hot shoe. Hot shoeing certainly permits you to go into a turn faster than you could otherwise. It does mean that you should not hot shoe unnecessarily. Find out how long you can go before you need to get that foot out. Then get it out and back on the pedal as quickly as you can. You must pedal your way to victory. Coasting does not win trophies.

Hot shoeing's partner on turns is riding the berm. The berm is the ridge of dirt thrown to the outside of the track by previous wheels running the track. This ridge can support your wheels and keep them from slipping out from under you on a tight turn. Riding the berm is a fast way around a corner.

Pros and Cons of Berm Riding

Since the berm is on the outside of the track, it is the farthest distance around the corner. So it may not be the best line through the turn. And if you do not know what you are doing, you may run right off the track.

However, if there is a jam on the inside, a skillful racer can often swing wide on the berm and pass slower riders. The faster speed permits him to make up the extra distance. This is especially true if there is a lot of following. Following is when the riders get in line instead of trying to get around each other.

This happens a lot, and there is no reason for it. When you follow along directly behind another rider or riders,

The inside rider is hot-shoeing to keep from falling. The outside rider is using the embankment and berm, keeping both feet on the pedals.

you are asking for trouble. If one falls, there is a domino effect on the others, and you are blocked off.

Why do riders follow? It may be that they are so worried about making the turn correctly that they are not paying enough attention to what the others are doing. They have picked out a line around the turn—possibly figured out in their practice runs—and now they are determined to stick to it no matter what the rest of the riders do.

In the case of a very bad hazard or rough, there may be only one best way through it. In such cases you might lose more by swinging wide than if you follow the leader. But such cases are rare indeed. When you follow the leader, you are letting him lead you into trouble and possible defeat.

A berm does not have to be a high ridge in order for it to help you. Even a small one can brace your wheel for a faster turn. You must learn by experience how fast and at what angle you can slide your wheels into the

This is following. Too many riders, intent upon taking the inside of the turn line up to make the corner, while the rider at the left swings wide to go around them all.

berm. In general, the correct way to do this is to turn your front wheel against it and let your back wheel slide into it. The back wheel will tend to do this anyway, because a rapid turn makes the back wheel want to slide.

You cannot practice berm riding too much, for cornering is where so many races are lost—and won.

Jumps

Jumping is fun, many riders report. The trouble with jumping is that it can be so much fun that a rider loses sight of the fact that he is not on the track to enjoy himself. He is out there to *win*. Taking off and sailing through the air provide a feeling that you don't get just from straight riding. While jumping has its place, you must remember that as long as you and your cycle are off the ground, you are not accelerating. You are coasting—losing speed. In order to pick up speed, you must have your wheels on the ground and your knobbies digging into the dirt.

The Right Way to Jump

Jumping is not dangerous—if done correctly. In some races you may see more spills on the turns than you will on the jumps. This may be because riders are more afraid of jumps than they are of corners and take more care.

It is very important that jumping be done correctly. The penalty for not doing it right can be more than just the humiliation of taking a hard spill yourself. You can easily bend a wheel, crack a frame, or bang up a fork. A jump can be harder on a cycle than any other part of a race.

The right way to make a jump is to pick up your front wheel and land on your back wheel. If you land on the front wheel first, you are likely to take a jolt that could send you scurrying for a new front wheel. It could also send you flying over the handlebars with the bicycle piling right on top of you.

Remember, there are three types of jumps: the downhill jump, the uphill jump, and the horizontal jump. These are described on page 60.

Jumping Technique

You can take a jump in one of three ways. One way is to slow down and ride over the bump—or down or up it, as the case may be. In this case, your wheels never leave the ground. This is the safest and surest method. It is also the slowest, and the flyboys are sure to leave you eating their dust.

On the other hand, those who charge gung ho into the jump, sail out into the air, and then bang down on the track are not doing so well either. This is because they are slowing down during the time their bike is flying. Also, the higher they fly, the harder they are going to hit—and this puts extra strain on the cycle frame, forks, and wheels.

The best technique for jumping is to split the difference between the too cautious and the too eager. In this way you go into the jump faster than Nervous Nelly, but you get back to pedaling faster than the imitation

Coming over a small downhill jump—in which you land at a lower level from which you took off—the rider on the left raised his wheel too high in the air. The rider on the right is getting his front wheel down first and is passing the other rider.

Evel Knievel. High jumps bring cheers from the crowd, but they slow down a racer.

Regardless of which type of jump it is, come into it pedaling for all you're worth. Don't slow down unless the track is rough or you get boxed in by other riders and must slow to keep from banging into them.

If you have watched yourself properly up to this point, you should not be boxed in. You should be in the clear and not following another rider too closely. A lot of beginners fall on the jumps. When you are in the air on a jump there is not a thing you can do about dodging somebody who has fallen in front of you. You are going to go down with him.

So Don't Follow is the first rule in jumping, just as it was in making a turn. The second rule is Go into the jump at the fastest speed you can. From your practice runs, you should have learned how much speed you can safely use in the jumps.

Flying

When your wheels are off the ground you are not progressing. You are coasting in the air. This would make it appear that jumping is not good, but that is not true. To keep your wheel on the ground when you go over a jump you have to slow down and press hard on your handlebars. This slows you down more than if you let her fly—provided you don't fly too high. Just let the cycle fly naturally. Don't try for an altitude record.

The right way to jump is to pedal like mad right up to the crest of the jump. Then shift your weight to the back of the cycle. This puts the center of gravity on the back wheel and lightens the front of the cycle.

At the same time pull up on your handlebars. This brings the front wheel up in a wheelie, and sets up the cycle so that you will make a back-wheel touchdown. You want the front wheel up, but not too high.

Now you are fully in the air. Both wheels are off the ground. You are coasting in the air and your speed will gradually drop until you can get your wheels back into action. Part of the reason for charging up the jump as fast as you can is to build up momentum to carry you through the jump with as little loss of speed as possible.

Avoiding a Back Flip

As I mentioned earlier, you do not want to get the front wheel up *too* high, because that delays you in getting it back on the ground. Even a split second's loss of time can harm you in such a short race. However, there is another very important reason for watching how high you raise the front wheel. If it gets too high, you and the cycle can do a back flip.

A back flip is funny to the spectators, but I have yet to see a rider chuckle when he does it. It is not funny to find yourself on your back in the dirt and the cycle riding you.

Danger of a back flip can be avoided by shifting your weight forward and pushing down on the handlebars if you are too high. You must be careful, however, not to overdo the correction. If you bring the wheel down too far, you risk the danger of a front wheel landing. A little experimenting will show you what is the best height to hold your wheel.

Riding the Air

Most riders stop pedaling when their wheels leave the ground. But sometimes—especially in big races—you will see the rider keep pedaling madly, as if his wheels were still on the ground.

As long as the wheels are off the ground, it might look as if the pedaling is not doing any good. Wouldn't the rider be better off grabbing a second's rest? No, he would not. The rider who keeps on pedaling even though both wheels are off the ground knows what he is doing.

As long as you continue to pedal, the back wheel is still spinning at top speed. When you touch that back wheel down, it will be going at that speed. There will be less jerk and slowdown when the moving wheel and the nonmoving earth contact each other.

It is the same as when you jump from a moving vehicle. If you land flat-footed, you are in great danger of falling. But if you land running as fast as you can, you go with your forward movement instead of fighting it. You are less likely to fall. Hitting the ground with fast-spinning wheels gains you another of those split-second advantages that add up to wins.

Tire Pressure

Landing from a jump is quite a bump for your tires. This brings up the problem of how much air pressure you should carry in them. This depends upon your weight, the weight of your cycle, the height you will be required to jump, and the like. So it is not possible to give a standard air pressure and say, "This is it." Try what you think is about right and if the tire flattens out too much on jumps, you increase the air pressure.

When you land on the back tire, it should give some. You don't want it too hard. The idea of pneumatic (air-filled) tires is to provide a springlike effect to help soften the ride.

But the tires shouldn't be too soft, either. If they compress too much when you come down on them, then the metal rim could cut into the tire. Right there you blow both the tire and the race.

A softer tire is good on turns. It tends not to slide out from under you as easily when you cut short. A softer tire also gives better traction, since it spreads out and gets more tire on the ground. Unfortunately, you still have the jumps and whoop-de-dos to consider. So the tire pressure you run must be judged by the jumps, so that you don't flatten the tire on landing.

Tire pressure will also depend upon the track conditions. This you can judge in your practice run. Then you can let some air out of the tires or pump them up before you begin actual racing.

Your weight will also have to be figured in. It is doubtful if you will ever run with less than 25 pounds of tire pressure. If you are heavy, you might go to as much as 35 or 40 pounds. But you will have to be the judge on this.

Touchdown

The second the back wheel touches the ground, shift your weight forward. You shoved it back on takeoff to help get the front wheel up. Now you want your weight forward. At the same time that you shift forward, push down on the handlebars to get the front wheel down.

It is absolutely essential that you keep your front wheel pointed straight ahead. Otherwise you may run into somebody else or run right off the track. You can also give yourself an upset if you get your front wheel crossed up when you land.

It is important to land with your front wheel straight. Here a rider—number 15—is having some trouble because his front wheel is not pointed down the track as he lands. This is a horizontal jump—that is, the riders land at the same level from which they took off.

You must be alert here, for spills are common. Also, BMX tracks are so short that the hazards are crammed in pretty close together. While you want to pick up speed as fast as possible after touching down, you may find yourself running into a turn right after you land.

A lot of riders fail to gauge their speed correctly. They are so anxious to get into high gear again that they go into the next turn too fast. This throws some of them high on the berm. Some of them even run right off the track because their speed is too fast for the sharper turns.

These quick turns right after a jump are another reason for getting that front wheel down fast. You cannot steer with the front wheel cocked up in the air.

Riding in Sand

If a course is a true motocross track, you will find sand and mud somewhere along its length. However, a lot of tracks have dropped both. Some courses are nothing more than winding trails with left and right turns, jumps, and maybe whoop-de-dos. Often the whoops are also omitted on junior tracks.

The excuse for these omissions is that the promoters want to make their tracks safer for everyone and easier for beginners. While they are certainly easier for beginners, it is doubtful that the promoters are doing a beginner any favors. If a beginner expects to go beyond this one track, he will find himself in rougher company as he advances in the sport. If he has not learned how to handle rough track conditions, he is going to find himself in deep trouble.

Take riding in sand, for example. Fortunately, the short length of a BMX track means that you will not have much of this. But it can upset you if you are not careful.

You have more of a problem with a bicycle in sand than with a motorcycle. The narrower tires of a bike sink into the sand more easily. The slower speed of a bike also causes the wheel to sink deeper into the sand.

Ride on Top

The secret of riding in sand is to stay on top of the sand as much as possible. Sand, being loose, not only lets you sink in, it also piles up in front of the wheel. And the loose grains drag at the tires.

All this means that the slower you go in sand, the more you dig in. Therefore, you want to cross a sandy stretch as fast as you can. One rider put it in this way: "I knew that you needed speed to cross sand. The way it was explained to me was that you want to move fast so there is no time for the wheels to sink in. But they neglected to tell me to keep my front wheel up. So I whammed into that stuff with all the pedal power I had. My front wheel sank in and I flipped right there."

The way to avoid this is to *hydroplane,* as motorcycle riders call it. Desert riders in particular are faced with lots of sand, and rarely have any trouble with it.

The secret is to shift your weight back on the seat as

you did in jumping. This weight shift puts more weight on the back wheel, and improves traction. At the same time it lightens the front wheel, which now wants to lift up. This is just what you want. In this way, the front wheel just skims the sand. It does not dig in or pile up a berm in front of itself.

The secret here is in the word "skimming." You do not want to do a wheelie. Just get the front wheel up enough that it will not dig into the sand. You do not have far to go and should roll right across without any trouble.

Loose Dirt

Loose dirt on the track is not the same as sand. A sand trap is usually deeper and the grains are finer. Loose dirt, kicked up by a lot of knobbies rolling around the track all day, presents an entirely different problem.

The ground may be hard underneath the layer of soft dirt. Here the loose dirt is not much of a problem if you are running straight. It can be a problem on turns, where it can cause your back wheel to slip out from under you.

You can counter this by making wider turns, slowing up or using a berm ridge to support your tires as you whiz around the turn. You must know the track conditions to judge properly what to do. These may change during the course of all-day racing. They may not be the same when you make your last moto as they were when you ran your first practice.

You can keep up with the changing track conditions by watching the other races while you are waiting for your time to come up again. After you get some experience at this sort of thing you can tell as much from watching the others as you can from running yourself.

Mud

More and more tracks are skipping this. Mud is hard on cycles—and hard on mamas who have to clean the riders' clothes after it is all over. It is not so hard on riders, for the stuff is soft to fall in.

Actually, riding through mud is not difficult unless it is very thin mud on top of a hard surface. In this case, it can be very slippery. Otherwise, if your tires can get traction, your knobby tires will pull you through the soup without a lot of difficulty.

Mud holes on a BMX track are usually made by running water into depressions on the track. This leaves a pretty soupy mess for the first riders. But the goo dries fast under a hot sun and soon the mud thickens enough to hold ruts. Then those who follow can ride in the ruts to a great advantage.

However, it is not a good idea to ride directly in the ruts of a rider in front of you. He could slip, and you'd be wiped out along with him. Unless the ruts were made by a rider in a previous race or by someone a good way in front of you, make your own ruts.

Another disadvantage of riding too closely behind another rider is that his knobby tires will be throwing mud right back in your face. It will pepper your goggles or helmet faceplate and you will not be able to see. If you are not wearing eye protection, the mud will get into your eyes, and that is worse yet.

Jumps into Mud and Water

Most mud hazards are set up so that you can just roll right into them. Occasionally a track promoter may want to make things harder for riders. He may put the mud in a drop so that you have to make a downhill jump into the goo.

In this case you proceed the same as in any other downhill jump. That is, you wheelie into it and land on your back wheel. Then drop your front wheel and pedal like mad to get out of the stuff. It is very important to keep your wheels absolutely straight. Any cross-up or landing at an angle will dump you for sure.

Riding in Water

It is very rare to find a track with a running-water hazard. This will happen only if there happens to be a stream cutting across the property.

You handle it the same way you would handle mud, but it is a lot more pleasant to dump into than the more messy goo. If the stream has a sandy bottom, you are in great shape. Wet sand is generally firm.

On the other hand, if the stream has a rocky bottom, you may be in trouble. Small rocks don't cause much bother. Your knobby tires will roll right over them. If there are larger rocks, they can cause you to slip if you don't hit them just right. Go over a big rock straight, and right down the middle. If you try to ride over the side of it, your tire will slip off.

10. Bike Care

BMX is harder on a bike than ordinary riding or racing. This means that bike care, always important, is even more essential in this sport. While proper maintenance and care will cut down your trouble and expense, you might as well face the sad truth: BMX racing is going to cost you money.

It is hard to say exactly what it will cost. Prices change all the time. At the time this is written (in early 1979) it costs about $500 to completely outfit one person for first class BMX competition. This includes a good bike, personal safety gear, and spare parts, which you always need at the track. It also includes memberships in associations and clubs. It does not include replacing a bike if you beat it to pieces with improper jumps and too many spills.

We are talking here of serious competition. A lot of riders get started with much less outlay. They may begin for $150 and build up. This is fine for a beginning, but if you are really serious, it is best to go first class right from the start. It is cheaper in the long run. One place where you should never try to economize is in safety gear. This is especially true of helmets.

Nor should you try to race a junk, third-hand bike. It

is dangerous and a handicap to winning. Buy good equipment and take care of it with proper maintenance.

Sponsorship

When the subject of the high cost of racing comes up, the interesting subject of sponsorship comes up along with it. Sponsorship means that some dealer or manufacturer is willing to help out on the cost.

In the best deal, the sponsor picks up all the costs, as well as sending you around the country to demonstrate his products at races you could never afford to attend yourself. This is really high living. A lot of beginners look upon such factory sponsorship as a latchkey to the gate of heaven. However, riding on a factory team is not an easy life. It is tough, and the pressure to win and keep winning is tremendous. After all, you are out there to show everybody that your sponsor's products are better than the competition's. You can't do this unless you can come in ahead of the pack a better-than-average number of times.

Local Dealer Sponsorships

Getting on a factory riding team is a dream only few will ever achieve, but any good rider can hope to be sponsored by a local dealer. You are not likely to get all the advantages you would get on a factory team, but sponsorship by even a small dealer will help cut your expenses. Besides, a good showing in such a sponsorship could be a stepping-stone to a factory sponsorship.

What can you expect from a local dealer sponsorship? Sometimes it means only that he will give you parts at wholesale prices. In others he may go further and provide you with the best bike he sells.

In some cases you don't have to be regularly sponsored to get some sponsor gravy. There are what are called "contingency prizes." In such cases a sponsor gives a prize, which may be anything from money to equipment, if the winner of a race is using that sponsor's products. Contingency prizes are posted in advance so that you know what is available and whether you can qualify.

What Sponsors Look for

Sponsors, of course, are looking for winners. You don't usually look for them. Just start winning races and they look for you.

However, you need a bit more on the ball than just the ability to win races for a sponsor to become really interested in picking up the tab for part or all of your racing expenses. Sportsmanship plays an important part in it. No dealer or company wants its products represented by a bum.

The sponsor also wants someone who can get along with the team. The bigger sponsors do not field and back single riders. They have riding teams. A prima donna does not fit into this kind of setup. There has been more than one case of a really good rider being bounced from a factory team because he could not get along with his fellow riders.

Another important point is the rider's ability to meet

and talk with people. This might seem far removed from pedaling around a track. However, consider such tours as the Schwinn cross-country swing. In addition to racing in important races—in hopes of bringing glory to the sponsors' products—the team also puts on exhibitions and instruction classes at various local dealerships. These are very important. They promote the entire sport as well as the team's products. The success of such demonstrations depends very heavily on the personalities of the racers on the factory team. At these seminars, personality is as important as is ability on the track.

What's in It for You?

If you are sponsored by a local dealer, you get whatever he can afford. This can range from giving you a cut on prices to providing you with a full racing bike which he maintains himself.

On a factory team, everything is furnished—and the furnishing is first class. Unless a race specifies stock bikes, your factory mount may well be a special job with features you won't find on the stock models. Sometimes the company will include improvements that it wants to test in action before putting them on the market.

There is no denying that the company works hard to give you an advantage. This does not necessarily mean you have a real advantage, because other, competing companies are doing the same with their riders. On this circuit, riders are bucking the best in the field all the time—and that includes the best in riders and the best in equipment.

The Other Side of the Coin

A sponsored rider has responsibilities, obligations, and restrictions that a lot of riders don't like. Some try this route and drop out. Others turn down the opportunity when it is offered to them.

The rider must observe the rules and restrictions that are laid down by the sponsor. These restrictions vary from one sponsor to the other. They are, however, the reason one rider turned down a dealer's sponsorship offer.

This was not a factory team offer. It was from a large dealer who was interested in advertising both his bikes and his repair shop. He also did a lot of modification work. He was especially interested in a winning rider who could demonstrate the superiority of the shop's custom work.

He did not offer a salary. He did offer to pay all expenses. This included a specially modified bike, all maintenance on it, and payment of all entry fees. He would also throw in a complete new outfit of riding clothes, for he wanted a sharp-looking rider who would be a credit to his business.

This sounds like a very good deal for a young rider on his way up. It could bring him to the attention of factory team captains, if he makes good. If this doesn't happen, it would still permit him to race in style at no expense to himself.

Independence

In this particular case the sponsor insisted upon retaining custody of the bicycle. Between races it was to be torn down completely, part by part, and cleaned and worked over by the sponsor's bicycle mechanics. He wanted the bike to run like a watch each time it raced. "This left me feeling like a hired hand," the rider said. "I was just supposed to do what I was told to do. They picked the races, got the bike ready, everything. Then I just pedaled for a few minutes a race, and my part was done.

"I want to make my own decisions, figure out my own strategy, ride when I want to ride and where I want to ride. I guess I'm too independent, but when I win a race it is all mine."

Not all sponsors are so demanding, of course, but all have their individual requirements. If you have the ability and money to back yourself, great. Otherwise, a sponsor sure helps with expenses.

BMX riders run mostly for trophies. The sport is just beginning to develop a professional class, and the financial rewards are small. Most riders are in it for the fun of it.

Basic Bike Care

By the time you get into racing you should already know something about caring for your bike. Unfortunately, few racers do it right. Racing, with its bumps and spills, is hard on a cycle. Just a cleaning and a quick once-over are not enough to keep a mount in racing condition.

A maintenance inspection starts with a thorough cleaning. There are two reasons for this. One, it removes dirt and grit that can cause wear in the moving parts of the bike. Two, it gets the crud off the bike so you can see hidden cracks and troubles.

Your postrace inspection should be as tough as the original tech inspection before the race. One winning rider said he goes over his bike after a race as if it were a secondhand bike he was going to buy from a dealer he did not trust.

Each part of the bike must be inspected. What you are looking for is anything that may slow you down or cause a breakdown in your next race. Waiting until race time is too late. There is no time to fix the trouble then.

Wheel Inspection

For the wheels, look to see that they have not been knocked out of line. Also look for dents in the rim. Check the spokes for proper tension and to see that they are evenly adjusted. Unevenly adjusted spokes can pull a rim out of line.

Turn the bike upside down. Remove the chain and spin each wheel. Does it turn freely and coast to a slow stop? This shows that there is no binding anywhere and that the bearings are good.

Bearings

Bearings are steel balls that roll around the axle to reduce hub friction. If the bearings are working right, the wheel will run straight without wobbling and will gradually coast to a stop. If the wheel wobbles, your rim may be bent. Or perhaps the bearings are worn or need adjusting. Old grease and dirt may have combined to

A smart rider realizes the value of proper bike care. Here one cleans and checks his wheel spokes after a race.

freeze the ball bearings so that they do not turn. What you need here is a quick disassembly, with thorough cleaning, adjusting, and regreasing.

Frame

The frame takes a beating in every race. Look it over carefully, sighting from the end to make sure that one of those spills did not bend the frame. Especially check the welded joints. Tiny cracks in the weld that you can hardly see can spread and dump you in the dirt after a hard jump.

Keep the paint in good condition, since it keeps down rust that can weaken the frame. Never repaint, however, without a careful check for cracks. The paint can hide some serious ones that may cause you trouble later.

While you are examining the frame, give the same careful check to the forks, and to the bolts that hold the axles to the frame. Don't overlook anything.

Brakes
Not enough riders pay proper attention to their brakes. They seem to have the idea that they are on the track to *go* instead of stop. That's the general idea, of course, but a rider who uses his brakes in a smart manner can step out a little faster than the competition. He can go into sharp turns at a faster speed, then just at the right point brake to the exact speed his experience tells him is right to get around the corner in the fastest time and avoid a wipeout.

Coaster brakes that work by reversing the pedals and caliper brakes that squeeze against the wheel from two sides have been popular on bikes for years. Recently Schwinn introduced a drum brake that team riders say is smoother and more efficient. It works by pressing brake shoes to the inside of the back hub. Its construction is said to be identical to motorcycle brakes.

Sprockets and Cranks
Sprockets require close care. Glance down their length to make sure that none have been bent. Look for worn

teeth. Wear may be caused by an out-of-line chain. If teeth are worn or bent, the sprocket wheel should be replaced.

The rear sprocket is held in place by a snap ring. You remove the back wheel and use a screwdriver in a slot to snap the ring out—making sure, of course, that it does not snap in your face. Then remove the sprocket wheel, slip on a new one, and replace the snap ring.

The front sprocket is a little more complicated, since you have to remove the pedals, chain, and crank. Since this is a book on racing and not bicycle repair, we don't have room to go into all details. There are books on bicycle repair in most libraries. You should familiarize yourself with them.

In checking the front sprocket, look for the same things you inspected in the rear one. These are worn teeth and alignment and wheel wobble. Spin the crank with the chain in place to check chain alignment and binding (jamming). Then remove the chain so you can check the sprocket for worn or bent teeth and any wobble. If the crank does not spin freely, it should be disassembled and cleaned. Binding is usually caused by dirt in the assembly.

How the Chain Works

The bicycle chain is out in the open. It must be lubricated to keep its rollers turning and to prevent undue wear on the sprocket teeth. This makes the chain a natural dust trap. It constantly picks up grit that acts like sandpaper to wear the parts.

A chain is really a group of roller bearings held together by plates. Rivets or pins go through the center to the sides of each roller and attach them to the plates. The pins act as axles for the rollers. The plates, in addition to joining the rollers together in a chain, act as hinges to make the chain flexible. This permits the chain to flex around the sprocket teeth.

When a sprocket tooth fits into the space between the chain rollers and pushes on the rollers to make the chain move, the rollers act as bearings. They turn inside the chain. This reduces wear on the chain by cutting friction between the chain and the sprocket teeth. Also the rollers make the chain itself move more smoothly. Without these rollers the bike would be harder to pedal and the chain would wear out faster.

The rollers jam when dirt and thickened grease grip them. Then friction and wear increase. The bike becomes harder to pedal and you will soon have sprocket trouble.

Chain Lubrication
Regular grease and oil are dirt sponges for chains. Fortunately, manufacturers have come up with what are called "dry" lubricants. These lubricants are compounded to pick up a minimum of dirt. They come under various trade names, such as *Slip-Spray, WD-40,* etc. They have a silicone base.

The chain should be removed from the cycle for a thorough cleaning before it is lubricated. Spraying the chain with a solvent while it is still on the cycle is no

good. For one thing, you don't get to the grit between
the rollers. Also, the powerful solvent may splatter on
other parts of the cycle and eat the paint off.

Proper Chain Cleaning

One of the links in a bicycle chain is the *master link*. It
is easy to spot. It is the largest link in the chain. Sometimes it is shaped differently from the others.

To remove the master link, snap off one of the side
plates. Doing this separates the chain so you can take
it off the two sprockets. Then put the chain in a can of
solvent and let it soak clean. It should be carefully
folded when placed in the cleaner. Jamming it in may
cause kinks that will cause sprocket wear when the
chain is put back on the bike.

After cleaning, inspect the chain carefully. Flex the
links. If there is still dirt inside, you will feel the grit
rubbing. If you do, back it goes in the soup for another soaking.

Adjusting the Chain

Chains, as any rider should know, need slack. If they
are too tight, there will be too much wear on both the
chain and the sprockets. The required amount of slack
is about ½ inch up-and-down movement in the center of
the chain.

This is for bikes without suspension. Now that we are
beginning to see suspension class entries, this ½-inch
slack may not be enough for spring-loaded wheels. This
is because the rear suspension permits more movement

of the back wheel. This can put heavy strain on the chain if you do not allow extra slack. It might even break the chain.

You can loosen or tighten the chain by loosening the back axle nuts and moving the wheel either forward or backward until the chain has the right tension.

If it is still not tight enough, then you may have to remove a chain link. While most repair work should be left to an expert, removing or replacing a chain link is a simple job that even a beginner can do. It takes a rivet tool which you can get at a bike shop. This is nothing more than a clamp that slips over the link. Then you screw down on a plunger that pushes out the rivet.

11. The Next Turn in the Track

The present age limits in bicycle motocross are from five to nineteen. This means that no matter how good or how bad you are, or how much you love the sport, the future is limited. The question then is: Where do you go from here?

The answer is: Into other types of two-wheel motor racing. And the natural progression is into motorcycles. I say this is natural because it was motorcycle motocross that provided the inspiration for BMX in the first place. The sport began with kids trying to use their bikes to ape motorcycles. So what is more natural than a BMX rider's stepping up to motorcycle motocross?

The Differences

Although BMX promoters claim that BMX is a pedal-power version of motorcycle motocross, there are many differences. In motorcycle motocross, the tracks are longer. The motos are run on a time basis and may be as long as thirty minutes at a time. The tracks are rougher and call for a tougher rider. You are moving faster, so you need faster reaction time. Motorcycle motocross is more dangerous. And it will cost you a lot more to race.

The cost can be offset because motocross, in contrast to BMX, is now thoroughly professional and a top rider can make money at it. This is because motorcycle motocross has become a big-time spectator sport. Like BMX, it started out primarily as a participant sport, but now it is often a major show.

This ad is for the 1978 Superbowl of Motocross, held in the Los Angeles Coliseum: "This classic motor race of the summer features a 70-mph superstraight, hairpin curves, ruts, bumps [whoop-de-dos], a diabolical water hole, and a shocking 150-foot leap from the top of the Coliseum to the football field. Eight of the best stadium racers are competing in the most important leg of the $400,000 AMA [American Motorcycle Association] sectional series championships. An evening's entertainment for all the family!"

This is quite different from looping a BMX track with pedal power. And it is also quite different from what motorcycle motocross was ten years ago. At that time it was a participants' sport, drawing only those who wanted to ride. Now a race like the Los Angeles Coliseum race may draw over 60,000 spectators.

Other Bicycle Racing Sports

No motorcycle or other two-wheel sport in America outdraws motocross today. So when you are ready to step up, this is the way to go.

However, if you do want to stick to bicycles, you can find bicycle racing in this country. Usually it is restricted to road or track racing. Track racing, as the name implies, is run on a prepared track. Since there are not many bicycle tracks, these races are usually run on automobile tracks. The cycles used are the lightest possible. The smooth tracks do not require as strong a cycle as BMX.

Since riders race around an oval track, these races lack the variety of BMX. So they are sometimes varied. One example is pursuit racing. Here the entrants are split into two groups. Half start on one side of the track. The other half start on the opposite side. The racers then try to catch up with each other.

Then there are matched sprint races. Here two riders are matched against each other.

There is still another kind of bicycle racing that is based upon elimination. The last person to cross the finish line in each heat drops out of the race. Heats continue to be run until only one rider—the winner—remains.

Road Racing

Road racing uses regular roads for tracks. Highly popular in Europe, it does not enjoy a wide following in the United States. Since the course leads over various kinds of terrain, multispeed bicycles are necessary for bicycle road racing.

Road racing is a tough, hard grind and requires strength and stamina. These races may vary from a few miles in length to the king of them all, the Tour de

France, which extends for 2,600 miles over the French countryside.

If you are really interested in bicycle road racing, you can do it in the United States—although the races are much, much shorter in length than the Tour de France. Try asking at bike shops for the addresses of bicycle clubs and associations that may sponsor road-racing schedules.

There are a lot of bicycle touring clubs around. While they don't sponsor road racing themselves, their members generally know what is going on in national bicycling. They can often fill you in on where to go for all kinds of cycle racing.

Motorcycle Racing Sports

The lack of interest in bicycle racing—except for BMX —generally sends BMX graduates into motorcycle sports. While motocross is the logical goal for the step up from BMX, there are a number of motorcycle racing sports a BMX rider can get into.

A popular form of motorcycle racing is dirt track. This may be an oval track race or a road race. In oval track, it is on a closed circular track—usually a horse racecourse. If the course is straight, then it is called a straight dirt track race. If the course is less than 2,250 feet, then it is called a short track race. These dirt track races are popular at county fairs.

Dirt track races were the most popular motorcycle competitions until motocross came along.

Dirt track racing is just one of many different types of wheeled sports that a BMX rider can graduate into as he grows older.

TT Races

TT—Tourist Trophy—races are very popular two-wheel events. TT is a race over a prepared course. It differs from oval track in that it has both left and right turns. In oval track racing all turns are to the left. A hill or jumps are included in the TT track, but the other hazards you find in motocross are missing here.

TT racing began in 1907 on the Isle of Man, and was one of the most rugged races ever run on motorcycles.

The curious name Tourist Trophy came into being as sarcasm because visiting riders kept winning the trophy from local cyclists.

Road Racing

Road racing is being run more and more on special off-road courses because authorities won't permit old-fashioned road races much anymore. One of the most popular of these used to run right down the main street of Elsinore, California, and was quite an affair. The road-racing machines, with their colorful paint and brilliantly garbed riders, provided a very colorful show.

Desert Racing

Here is another type of two-wheel sport you can graduate to. However, desert racing may be a dying sport. It has always been limited to western areas where there is desert. But increasing environmental concern is seriously limiting this type of off-road racing.

The great Barstow, California, to Las Vegas, Nevada, desert run once pulled as many as 3,000 entrants. When they charged off across the desert, their knobby tires literally raised a dust storm.

Unfortunately, desert terrain is slow to recover from such punishment. It generally takes as much as ten years for ground cover to replace itself. As a result, racing across public land has been severely curtailed.

Desert racing still manages to hold on, however. It is kept alive by looping courses into smaller, privately owned areas. As this is written, there is a 400-mile race called the Mint 400 still being run near Las Vegas.

Desert racing on a motorcycle is tough on bike and rider. You are faced with sand, hard adobe, gullies, rocky areas, hills, cacti, and even rattlesnakes.

It takes a skilled and determined rider to come in first in this kind of race.

Enduros

An enduro is a race for those who do not care for break-neck speed. Before the race a pathfinder lays out the course. He marks checkpoints along the way and his own time between the points. Each rider then must try to come as close to this pathfinder's time as possible. The course is off road and through any kind of terrain, from streams to hills and rocks.

In enduro, you are racing the clock rather than your fellow riders. You keep one eye on your odometer and the other on a clock. You must come into each check-point exactly on the second—if you can. You start with 1000 points and you lose points each time you reach a checkpoint late or early.

Then, in addition to these "known checks," there are "secret checks." These extra checks are thrown in to make sure everyone maintains an average speed. You lose one point for every minute you are late to the secret check, and two points for every minute you are early.

And you can't beat the early penalty by stopping when you see a secret check and letting the clock tick away. Once the checker sees you—and that is when you see the checker—you are timed right then.

They have some other cute rules to erase points on you, but I don't have the space to go into them. I'll just say that a lot of riders who have always depended on speed find themselves really working in this kind of race. It is much harder and more fun than it first appears.

Observed Trials

Observed trials is another two-wheel sport that does not involve speed. While ordinarily done on motorcycles, it can be adapted for bicycles as well.

The rules say that a trials course is laid out through a series of natural obstacles. In practice, these are often man-made obstacles that ape natural hazards.

This means you will be riding in mud, water, and sand, across logs, over rocks, up and down ditches, and anything else that a bike or motorcycle can get over. Oh, yes, you can always get over the hazard. The rules require that the person who laid out the course ride it three times himself to prove that it can be done. This effectively prevents him from getting too nasty. However, if the trailblazer is a real expert, he can make things really tough for the common herd of rider.

How Trials Work

You can ride the trials course as fast or as slowly as you wish. At the beginning you are given a number of points. Each time you *dab*—that is, you put your foot down to balance the cycle—you lose some points. If you hot shoe, fall, or go out of bounds, more points are erased.

The secret of trials riding is control and balance, skill and coordination. Although it is run at slow speed, many agree that trials riding is more difficult to do properly than any of the speedier cycle sports. In fact, *Dirt Bike* magazine recommended trials riding for beginners in motorcycle motocross as a means of learning to control their bikes in difficult situations. The magazine said, "Young riders who intend to start competing in motocross are advised to complete a season of trials, as it is an excellent way to learn to ride on muddy surfaces, stony ground, and off-camber, rugged terrain."

A lot of riders agree with this. Trials force a rider to move carefully and to analyze every hazard.

Motocross

While all of these motorcycle sports are interesting, a BMX rider graduating out of his sport mainly has his eye on motorcycle motocross.

A BMX rider must realize, of course, that he is coming into a new sport. It is not the same as BMX with a motor added. There are a lot of differences—enough to send you back to riding school again. However, BMX experience gives you a tremendous advantage over a beginner in motorcycle racing who has not been in BMX. The BMX rider has learned track sportsmanship, the basic rules of motocross, and general techniques.

Racing techniques are basically the same for both sports, but you will find things complicated by the faster speed and mechanical differences of the motorcycle.

Motorcycle motocross is the top two-wheeled sport today. Here one wave takes off on a moto while a second one rolls up to the starting line.

Jumping is an example of how the two sports are alike, but still different.

The Power Difference
You jump the same way. That is, you come in as fast as you can, lift up the front wheel, and touch down on the back wheel. You make sure your front wheel is pointed down the track when you land.

The big difference in motorcycle jumping is in handling your extra power. You cut your power as your wheels leave the ground in cycle racing, and turn it back on just before your back wheel touches down. This is to prevent the motor racing too fast during the jump. You are going faster than in BMX and you have to react faster.

Also, you stand on the pegs. You do not jump sitting down. This is so you can shift your body to keep the cycle balanced and lined up properly.

Just as your back wheel touches down, you turn on the power, bring the front wheel down, and get ready to brake fast if a turn comes up.

In comparing this with a BMX jump, you can see that most of it is just what you learned in your bicycle jumps. The big difference is in how you handle your power. You have to learn to open and close your throttle at the proper times.

The difference between the power of a motorcycle engine and the leg power of your pedals forces you to react faster. When you open the throttle on a motorcycle, you have to be prepared for fast action. The feel and the "jump" of a motorcycle must be learned before you race it.

This and the way you handle your body in controlling the cycle are not difficult to learn. The differences cause trouble for beginners because at first they try to ride the cycle the same way they rode their BMX bicycles. The weight, speed, and throttle are so different that they become confused.

Motocross Schools

The best possible preparation for shifting from BMX to motocross is to attend a motocross school. Special schools and seminars in proper riding techniques are sponsored by various motorcycle companies. Also, sometimes well-known riders teach independent schools.

In addition to these schools, a lot of cycle clubs and associations conduct their own seminars. Schools such as these will give you the fine tuning you need to move up to this faster sport.

Growing up with BMX

But in the meantime, there is today with BMX. You have one advantage here, in that this is a new sport. It is still being formed, changing each year as new ideas and new equipment come into play. From a few riders trying to use bicycles to ape motorcyclists back in 1972, the sport has grown until more than 80,000 boys and girls are participating in it.

And this, they tell us, is just the beginning. Most sports are well established, with histories going back for years and sometimes centuries. But BMX, being something entirely new, gives you an opportunity to grow up with it. In this way you do more than just ride for fun and trophies; you are actually helping form the sport itself, working out the bugs, and really pioneering.

Glossary

Berm: A ridge of dirt piled up on the outside of a dirt track by sliding cycle wheels.

Cherry picking: Entering a race below one's classification or age in hope of winning an easy trophy.

Gear numbers: A chart of numbers that tells you what size sprockets to use to achieve various gear ratios. Gear number charts may be found at most dealers. See *Gear ratios.*

Gear ratios: The gear ratio of a bicycle is the quotient of the number of teeth on the front sprocket, which is attached to the pedal crank, divided by the number of teeth on the rear sprocket. The gear ratio tells you how many times the rear wheel will revolve for each single revolution of the pedals.

Hot shoeing: Sliding one foot along the ground to keep from upsetting your bike on turns.

Knobbies: Tires with a heavy, knoblike tread used in racing.

Lacing: The placement of spokes in a wheel; also the act of placing spokes in a wheel.

Moto: One lap around the track in bicycle motocross. In motorcycle motocross, a predetermined amount of time during which riders attempt to complete the most laps.

Nipple: Nut used for tightening wheel spoke tension.

Riders' meeting: Group meeting at which race rules are explained.

Sanctioned race: Race run under an association's authorized rules.

Wheelie: The stunt of running on the back wheel with the front wheel raised in the air.

Whoop-de-do: A rough section of track.

Index